# HOPE
## *When You're*
# HURTING

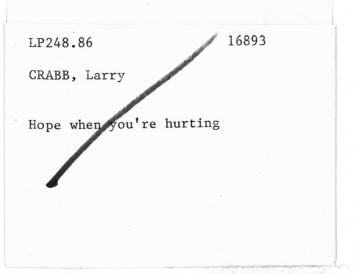

Also by Dr. Larry Crabb available in
Large Print from Walker & Company

*Finding God*

Answers to Four Questions
Hurting People Ask

# HOPE
## *When You're*
# HURTING

## Dr. Larry Crabb
## & Dr. Dan Allender

Walker & Company
New York

Large Print edition published by arrangement with Zondervan Publishing House

First Large Print edition published in the United States of America in 1999 by Walker Publishing Company, Inc.

Published simultaneously in Canada by Fitzhenry and Whiteside, Markham, Ontario L3R 4T8

All Scripture quotations, unless otherwise indicated, are taken from the *Holy Bible: New International Version*®. NIV®. Copyright ©1973, 1978, 1984 by International Bible Society. Used by permission of Zondervan Publishing House. All rights reserved.

**Library of Congress Cataloging-in-Publication Data**
Crabb, Lawrence J.

Hope when you're hurting : answers to four questions hurting people ask / Larry Crabb & Dan Allender.
    p.    cm.
Includes bibliographical references.
ISBN: 0-8027-2744-1 (pbk.)

1. Pastoral counseling.  2. Hope—Religious aspects—Christianity. 3. Consolation. 4. Large type books. I. Allender, Dan B. II. Title. III. Title: Hope when you are hurting.

[BV4012.2.C67   1999]
253.5—dc21                                      99-31860
                                                    CIP

Printed in Canada
10  9  8  7  6  5  4  3  2  1

# Contents

❧

# PART 3
## What Will the Helper Do?

# PART 4
## What Can I Hope For?

# Acknowledgments

⚜

THANKS TO:

The Zondervan team, especially our capable editor and good friend, Sandy Vander Zicht.

Sealy Yates, literary agent and brother in Christ, a special friend.

Diane Vartuli, Susan Berthiaume, and Laura Wackman (personal assistants of Larry and Dan respectively), hard workers, devoted colleagues, and wonderful friends.

Our communities of fellow journeyers, too numerous to mention: without their stimulation our ideas would never take shape.

Our wives, Rachael (Larry) and Becky (Dan), whose belief in what we do and patience as we do it means more than they can possibly know.

# A Word to the Reader

⚮

MY VIEWS ON COUNSELING are changing. That's what I think. But not everyone
agrees with that assessment. Many friends
and former students think I'm just becoming clearer on what I've always believed and
have taught for years. Some of them wonder whether I've recently found the courage
to speak up more boldly and whether I'm
mistaking new courage for new ideas. Others don't believe I've changed at all, but think
I should.

The direction my mind is now taking
fits comfortably with the slogan I attached
to my ministry twenty years ago: "Meeting
counseling needs through the local church."
And an irrepressible call from God has stirred
me deeply. Like an insecure kid playing bas-

ketball, I've not always wanted the ball passed to me. Now I'm more resolved than ever to position myself to catch whatever ball God throws my way and take it to the basket. I may not score, but I will shoot. That does feel like new courage.

Still, I can't shake the conviction that something different is rattling around in my head, something that cannot be fully explained by increased clarity or a stiffer backbone. For twenty-five years, I've puzzled over people's problems, mine included. I've wondered how those of us who accept Christianity as a comprehensive worldview should think about our personal troubles and best go about helping each other.

And I've come up with a framework for thinking through these questions, a framework I've presented in books and classes and seminars for a long time. Like a house you live in for years, it's often needed remodeling, sometimes extensive, but I've never thought about tearing it down and building another. I still haven't. I like it. I believe it's been constructed according to biblical blueprints.

But something is happening that I did not anticipate and am at a loss to explain. New winds are blowing, both across our culture and deep in my soul. The wind I can feel in me is not violent. It is not destroying the old house I've lived in for so long, but it is lifting it off its pilings and carrying it to unfamiliar ground.

In a sentence, let me tell you what I mean: The ideas I've developed have done far more to guide counselors in their professional work (the old pilings) than to connect Christians together in healing community (to many, unfamiliar ground). I'm grateful for whatever help I've been to professional counselors as they do their good work. But that's not been my dream. I've wanted to help meet counseling needs through the local church, through communities of God's people relating meaningfully and healingly to one another as together they search for God.

From my current vantage point, hanging out the window as the house soars above changing landscapes, the direction I'm being taken seems new, revolutionary, radical. The notion that caring Christians could do a better job helping people in natural community than in professional offices is largely untested. I want to see that changed.

And I'm hopeful. I'm flying over brown desert right now, but I can see lush meadows on the horizon, meadows where the waters are still and the pastures green, good places for troubled people to be nourished, taste joy, and find rest.

Dan Allender, longtime friend and colleague, is sharing the writing responsibilities with me. He wrote chapters 8, 9, 10, 11, and 14. His ideas, too, are undergoing refinement in the furnace of his relentlessly inquisitive and razor-sharp mind. For the most part, our emerging viewpoints fit together nicely. But in a few areas, some important, we may be heading in different directions. Those differences will become clear as you read our book, particularly Part 4.

We invite you to read our words in the same spirit we wrote them, with confident hope that there is living water for parched throats and heavenly bread for empty stomachs.

Our souls were not meant to exist on a diet of boredom, misery, and terror. God provides another dining room where we are invited to delight in the richest of fare. The hope is that we'll get a few more servings from that menu now that will keep us going strong until we find complete delight at the heavenly banquet table forever.

# HOPE
## *When You're*
# HURTING

# 1

# Four Questions
# Hurting People Ask

⁓◈⁓

I ARRIVED A FEW minutes before noon. Brian was already there, sitting by himself in a dark corner of the crowded restaurant, nervously tapping the fingers of his left hand on the table, his right hand holding his chin.

We began with a few pleasantries, ordered lunch, then spent a few minutes catching up. We talked about the usual sort of stuff—job, health, the Denver Broncos. We hadn't seen each other for nearly a month.

Then, with a noticeable sigh, Brian let me know he was ready. For what, I wasn't sure. When he called asking to meet me for lunch, I felt his urgency.

His eyes dropped to the spoon he had just picked up. In a flat voice, he said, "Mary's going to leave me."

> Speaking the truth in love does not give anyone license to share whatever he happens to think or feel.

A familiar sadness washed over me. I'd been here before. I've heard words of confusion and despair a thousand times.

When I was in private practice, I heard heartbreaking stories every day, one after the other. The suffering took its toll. I'm no longer in practice, but I still talk and share and listen. The stories keep coming, and hearing them has not gotten easier.

I never know exactly what to say. In many ways, I feel more adequate writing about counseling than doing it. The notion that trained therapists select their words according to a well-established scientific plan, like surgeons choosing where to cut, is an illusion.

Sometimes I just sit there and look at the people I am counseling. Maybe I'm trying to connect with who they are and where they are since I can't change what they're going through. Sometimes I look away. Connecting with them can be too heavy a weight to bear.

At the lunch table with Brian, I joined him in staring at his spoon. I knew Mary. I didn't like her. She struck me as an angry woman, hiding her fangs behind an unconvincing smile. I feared what would happen if I crossed her.

Whether therapist or friend, you can't always say what occurs to you. Speaking the truth in love does not give anyone license to share whatever he happens to think or feel. When Brian told me Mary was going to leave him, my immediate thought was "Good! I don't know how you've endured that woman for this long."

I chose not to share my thoughts. But I wasn't sure what I should say. I wanted to be authentic, helpful, and compassionate, but words that satisfied those criteria didn't jump out at me. Wisdom comes slowly, but I've learned that it comes more often when I tune in to my passion to connect with hurting people instead of trying to figure them out.

Connection, not analysis, seems closer to the center of my work.

Doctors diagnose, then prescribe. So do plumbers and car mechanics. But counselors relate, more like friends than our professionalism allows us to admit, and more like pastors than our billing habits suggest. We're people who pour the fullness of ourselves into the emptiness of another. Unfortunately, sometimes our souls don't feel very full.

> **Connection,**
>
> **not analysis,**
>
> **seems closer to**
>
> **the center of**
>
> **my work.**

"What led up to this, Brian?" I asked, not because I thought it was a good question. I just wanted to know.

"Mary and I have never been close. You know that, Larry. We've had a lousy marriage for years. If it weren't for the kids, I'd probably have left her a long time ago. You've never seen her when she blows up. It's unbelievable. I cannot please the woman, and I've never known how to reach her. I've pretty well given up, but there's the kids. I don't know what to do." His eyes returned to the spoon.

I still didn't know what to say. My initial confusion had advanced to a sharp feeling of inadequacy. I wished he were talking to Mother Teresa. With all those wrinkles that only compassion can produce, surely she'd know what to say.

Maybe he needed to tell all this to a professional. That was my next thought, which lasted for the second it took me to remind myself that I was a professional, highly trained, properly licensed, with a reputation as an effective therapist.

Funny how quickly my mind shifted from Brian needing a godly person like Mother Teresa to his needing a trained expert.

But maybe that makes sense. Like most people, when things go wrong I want someone who knows what he's doing to fix it.

I remember years ago when our eight-year-old son Kenny was delirious. His fever measured 105 degrees. He was babbling nonsense like the chronic schizophrenics I worked with in locked wards of mental hospitals. He didn't recognize his mother or me.

I panicked. Was his brain damaged? Would he ever be normal again? Like Brian, I wanted help. Not knowing what to do, I wanted answers from someone who did, so I called our doctor.

Did my doctor feel the same inadequacy talking to me that I felt listening to Brian? I don't think he did. His medical degree better equipped him to advise a father distraught over a feverish son than my psychology degree prepared me to counsel a man whose wife was talking divorce.

I distinctly recall how good I felt when the physician took immediate charge. He asked specific questions, gave clear and firm directions, and assured me our son would be fine. We did what we were told, and Kenny fully recovered.

**When we hurt, we ask questions. And we insist that someone be able to answer them.**

As I talked with Brian, I knew that despite my doctorate in clinical psychology, I wasn't the same kind of expert for personal problems as my physician was for physical ones. Something was different, and at that moment I wasn't sure I was an expert at all. But Brian wanted to believe I was.

That's to be expected. When any of

us run into trouble we can't handle, we want to find someone with solutions. It's comforting to ask questions of people who have answers. It's maddening when they don't. When we hurt, we ask questions. And we insist that someone be able to answer them.

Maybe that's why we've convinced ourselves that counselors are experts. Isn't that what the framed diploma and the state license mean?

We live in an era of experts. We keep a list of emergency numbers visible near our telephones because experts do exist. Plumbers open drains that we can't. Dentists relieve toothaches that otherwise would keep us awake all night. Delirious children get better under medical care when without it they might die.

But somewhere along the line, we've gotten the idea that expert help should be available to do for our troubled lives what it can do for clogged drains, aching teeth, and fevered bodies. We have questions, and we want someone to have the answers. When we hurt, we want help.

In this book, we will take a look at what it means to "get help" for personal problems. When we struggle with difficulties in our

7

lives that we can't manage, we ask four basic questions:

1. What's wrong?
2. Who can help?
3. What will the helper do?
4. What can I hope for if I do seek help?

We explore the kinds of answers that folks in our modern culture come up with, ranging all the way from "I'm okay. A little more discipline, and I'll be fine" to "There is no hope for me unless I get professional help."

How we answer those four questions determines what we do and where we go to find help when we hurt. During our lunch, Brian shared a long-kept secret. "I was homosexually raped when I was eleven. Could that be what's wrong with me? Is that why I've never been able to relate to Mary?" That was Brian's tentative answer to the first question, **What's wrong with me?**

He continued, "I'm telling you all this because you're more than a friend. You're a psychologist. I figure you'll know what to do." This was his reply to the second question: **Who can help?**

From watching television talk shows and

sitcoms, Brian had some idea of what would happen if he "entered therapy." "I guess we'd talk a lot about my childhood. Maybe I'd cry for the first time in years," he said. He had a few answers to the third question, **What will a helper do?**

Toward the end of our lunch, he thoughtfully commented, "You know, I've never been really close to anyone. Never. Maybe getting some counseling would free me up to make real friends, maybe meet a woman I could really relate to." That was Brian's hope, his answer to the last question, **What can I hope for?**

I don't believe any one of Brian's answers is correct. Is it possible that most people in our culture come up with wrong answers to these important questions? Do the answers we give take us away from the real hope that is available? If so, are there better answers that would open the door to new hope? Are joy and peace and self-control really available, even if your spouse leaves you, or you feel like a failure, or your history includes abuse?

We think so. And it's with that hope we write this book.

# PART

# 1

# What's Wrong?

# 2

# Why Am I Still Struggling So Much?

❦

FATIGUE IS A REGULAR part of my life, an unwelcome companion that I wish would go away. Usually I manage to push on and do what I have to do. Occasionally a burst of energy swoops in like a tornado and I feel great. More often, I get so tired I just sit. Then I tend to feel lazy and berate myself for not getting to all that remains undone.

Why am I so often so tired? Do I have chronic fatigue syndrome? Am I anemic? Blood tests tell me I'm healthy. Can they be trusted? Is improved nutrition and rigorous exercise the answer? Maybe prescribed "uppers" would help.

13

Sometimes I wonder if the problem is demonic harassment. Are there "fatigue demons" that have been sent to keep me from carrying out my mission?

Perhaps I'm just lazy, an undisciplined slug who needs to stop whining and get busy. Or could it be unconfessed sin? King David didn't do too well emotionally when he pretended he had done no wrong. Should I rummage through my life in search of a sin I haven't confessed?

Then my mind (which I wish were more fatigued) scurries in a different direction. If I knew God better, then I could press on with the energy of an athlete to finish the race he has set before me.

But that doesn't always work. I know a few godly saints who have battled weariness and discouragement for years.

So what's the problem? What's wrong? Maybe a therapist could help. My inner self could be like a bucket with a hole in it through which my emotional energy is draining. The hole might be an inordinate need for approval or the constant self-imposed pressure to prove myself. If a therapist could identify the leak, then maybe together we could plug it up so the bucket would eventually get full.

# A DESPERATE SEARCH

What's wrong? I want to know. When we're hurting, we all want to know why. Knowing what's wrong is the first step toward finding a solution. If we can answer this first question, we feel hope. If we stay confused, frustrated by a problem with no clear explanations, we lose hope, and we think the problem will never go away.

The principle is worth more thought: the problems we face, even the big ones, aren't so bad. It's the unexplained ones that scare us to death. We're not nearly so bothered by the size of a problem as we are by its degree of mystery. It's not knowing what's wrong that arouses the worst terror. Mystery scares us because it puts us out of control and leaves us with an option we don't naturally like—to trust someone besides ourselves.

Perhaps that accounts for our desperate search for explanations. We want to know why we're so depressed, why our marriage isn't working. Once we know what's wrong, we feel back in control. If someone understands the problem, that person will know how to solve it. Knowledge is the key. Explanation becomes our hope. We don't need a person if we have a plan. Trust becomes unnecessary, a nice concept to talk about in church but one we don't have to practice in real life.

〜✦〜

**We're not nearly so bothered by the size of a problem as we are by its degree of mystery. It's not knowing what's wrong that arouses the worst terror.**

〜✦〜

When we run into a problem, it's our demand for explanation and control that prompts us to so quickly ask, "What's wrong?"

Many people are struggling with problems they have not yet been able to adequately explain. It's as if they're permanently trapped in that moment of terror before the doctor looks up from the lab report to tell them what's wrong. They've asked, "What's wrong?" but no one has answered. And that's scary. Unexplained problems bother us most.

Our search for explanations may not be entirely good. The demand to know what's causing our difficulties may actually be preventing us from finding a pathway through them toward joy. It may in fact keep a few unnecessary struggles alive and block the development of more productive ones.

Let me explain what I mean by making two points: first, some problems have no explanations, therefore we have no control over them. We really don't know what to do to solve them, and we never will. Second, our determination to explain what's wrong can become too strong. It can displace better passions.

## SOME PROBLEMS HAVE NO EXPLANATIONS

People can be divided into two groups: those who think that life works (or could work if certain principles were followed), and those who know it doesn't. No matter how scrupulously we obey the rules, life eventually throws us a curve we didn't expect and couldn't prevent. The second group knows that.

A good friend of mine, senior pastor of a large church, asks every applicant wanting a pastoral staff position the same question: "Do you believe life is manageable?" A "yes" answer instantly disqualifies the applicant. The pastor wants a team of associates who will manage what can be managed and trust God in the remaining chaos.

Many areas of life, of course, are manageable. We can profitably answer the "what's wrong" question in these areas and find practical solutions. As long as we stay there, asking only questions that can be answered and facing only problems that can be solved, life can move along pretty smoothly.

My wife, Rachael, read the account of a mother who was having a hard time rousing her young children out of bed on cold, winter mornings. That was her problem. Her desire to explain the problem was easily satisfied: the kids didn't like leaving the cozy warmth of heavily blanketed beds to put on chilly clothes that had hung all night in a poorly heated closet.

This creative mother found a simple solution. Have the children select their outfits for the next day, both under and outer, before they go to bed. Then early next morning throw every chosen garment into the dryer for a few minutes and place them on a chair near each child's bed. Quick movement from the bed to the chair was rewarded by the feel of warm clothes on skin that had no time to get cold. Problem solved.

That's how we think all of life should work: face a problem, find an explanation, come up with a solution. The difficult conclusion that honest people eventually reach is that only some of life works that way. An even more difficult conclusion is that it's often the most important parts that don't.

The tuxedoed groom and his gowned bride should be whisked away from the church to live happily ever after. Single folks should be able to find fulfillment in ministry or career, or find a mate. People suffering from depression should feel happy again.

And sometimes they do. But not always. Not even most of the time. We like to think that help is available, that we already know the principles to follow and the counselors to see that have the power to make things turn out as they should. We want to believe that society's job is matching needs with resources, getting the word out so people know what to do and can find someone who can help. It's comforting to assume that explanations for each of our problems have been figured out, or soon will be by teams of researchers huddled in their laboratories and that the explanations already in hand are enough to guide us through most problems.

That's certainly what we want. But

maybe that's not the way things are. What we want is not always available. C. S. Lewis once observed that when we discover desires within us that this world cannot satisfy, it should make us wonder if we were designed for another world. And if we entertain that possibility, we might also begin to wonder if what is wrong in this world will never really be fixed till we get to the next. Maybe the pie we most want, the pie we were meant to enjoy, really is in the sky.

## THE MYSTERIOUS
## REALM OF THE SOUL

It is difficult to stop trying so hard to explain everything. Explanations work well. They have proven themselves enormously useful in many areas, like building cars, fixing teeth, and wiring houses for electricity.

But the further we move away from things and toward people, the less useful explanations become. When we face personal struggles, when our problems involve tensions in relationships and trouble in our lives, efforts to explain and control have less value because these kinds of struggles take us away from the realm of matter, where things are relatively predictable, and into the mysterious realm of the soul.

Not everyone, however, agrees. Social scientists (the very term implies hope that science can understand sociability) regularly correlate types of backgrounds with sets of symptoms, trying to explain, for example, antisocial behavior in terms of such things as early abandonment. If something can be explained, perhaps it can be controlled. That's the hope. Autopsies are performed on dead marriages to determine the cause of death in order to come up with ideas that might keep other marriages alive.

ᄋᔕᄋ

**But the further we move away from things and toward people, the less useful explanations become.**

ᄋᔕᄋ

Christians indulge their urge for explanation in the way they approach not only the social sciences but also the Bible. We scour the text in search of a failproof system for raising kids, raising money, and raising sick people from their beds. We desperately and stubbornly want an orderly world that we can manage.

Now the effort to explain, predict, and

control how people function would make good sense if people were things, physical things like car motors or abstract things like economic systems. They aren't, of course, and that's why our relentless desire to explain them is frustrated. So we moderns have reduced the mysterious soul, the irreducible personal reality that defines our distinctly human existence, to a manageable self, a psychological entity that can be analyzed, experimented with, damaged, and repaired. We think we can do something to a self with roughly predictable results. A soul seems more elusive, random, more difficult to chart. We don't sense the need to stand silent, with curiosity and wonder, before a self. The idea of self allows us to do more.

But the soul is not so easily managed. It isn't a thing so much as an identity, a burst of energy housed in a body (and strangely related to it in an interactive way) that moves at the prompting of its own creative initiative.

B. F. Skinner was wrong: What is outside a person does not control him. The control panel is on the inside, and only the individual can reach his own levers. I cannot successfully manage you. And you'll do no better with me.

The soul can, of course, be studied, but never explained; nourished but not possessed; influenced by many forces outside of itself, but never entirely predicted. The soul is capable of connecting with other souls in ways that bring life to potential, but it cannot be controlled. A soul can be explored better than it can be explained.

When personal problems develop, those who understand that people are living souls more than manageable selves have a hard time with theories that leave no room for mystery. Reductionism, that scientific determination to reduce the unexplained to entirely rational categories, is offensive to them.

Psychological explanations arise out of

> The soul can be studied but never explained; nourished but not possessed; influenced by many forces outside of itself, but never entirely predicted.

the field of psychology's desire to cast it-self as a credible science in the tradition of chemistry and physics. Moral explanations, particularly those that look for identifiable sin behind every emotional struggle, are too pat. Biochemical explanations, of course, have their place, but people who believe in the soul are wary of efforts to explain too much with this category.

## A PROBLEM SOLVED

If some problems have no adequate expla-nations, and never will have, then we must come to grips with confusion and learn to live in mystery. A problem from my life il-lustrates this point.

From the time I was emerging out of the terrible twos until I was halfway through my twenties, I stuttered, sometimes badly. I remember so many times asking, "What's wrong? Why can't I talk like everybody else?" I wanted an explanation for my prob-lem that would show me how to solve it. Like most people since the Enlightenment, I assumed that someone could figure out what was wrong with me and could help me speak fluently. Despite visiting several speech thera-pists, I never found that person.

It made no sense. Sometimes I spoke

fine. Other times I blocked miserably. My tongue was properly attached to the back of my throat, allowing full range of movement (I remember checking); my teeth were where they belonged; and the muscles controlling lip movement worked well except when I tried to say words that began with those two dreaded letters "l" and "p." Then everything went wrong. My tongue either locked against the roof of my mouth, held there, it seemed, by super glue, or it wildly bounced up and down. My teeth clenched with enough force to loosen fillings, or they clattered in rhythm with my tongue. My lips either froze, or quivered uncontrollably. Either I blocked on a difficult word, making no noise beyond gasps and grunts, or I repeated its first letter a dozen times or so before the rest of it exploded out of my mouth.

I hated it. I tried to change, but I couldn't. The answer, if there was one, had to lie in knowledge. Something was clearly wrong, but I couldn't figure out what. The search for an explanation for my stuttering consumed me, even to the point of doing both my master's and doctoral research on stuttering.

When I tell others about my stuttering,

someone always asks the inevitable question: "You don't seem to have any problem with stuttering now. How did you get over it?"

They expect a rational answer, one that might help their child or friend with a similar problem. I always disappoint them.

> The saints among us are not especially interested in explanations.

"An older, crusty psychologist, one of my supervisors in graduate school, heard me stutter one day. He looked at me the way a drill sergeant would look at a recruit who collapsed after ten pushups. Then he said, 'I used to do that. Yeah, real bad, worse than you. Then I got fed up with it, so I stopped. Been stuttering for years, right? It's about time you stopped, too. You ought to be sick of it by now!'"

From that moment, something changed. I still stuttered but less frequently and severely. I felt new hope that I could stop. Over the next five or six years, the problem slowly disappeared. I stopped stuttering. In the past twenty years, I may have mildly stuttered a half dozen times.

Don't try to figure out the "therapeutic element" in what the psychologist said to me. That's how new systems of psychotherapy get started. But that's what we want to do. We want to understand what happened so we can make it happen again, with someone else who stutters. We want to reduce mystery to a usable system. Mystery requires us to connect with someone, to trust. System allows us to follow a plan, to control.

Our culture rebels against the idea that some problems are beyond understanding. The modern seminar industry is built on that rebellion: six steps to this, the secret of that, guaranteed principles to help you achieve what you want. We're working feverishly to abolish mystery from culture. As a result, we're losing our sense of wonder; we don't want to feel the dangerous excitement of facing an unknown tomorrow. Getting past our demand for explanation and accepting mystery is no small achievement.

The saints among us are not especially interested in explanations, although they pursue them where available. Where elements of life are confusing, they are content to live with mystery. And that's my second point.

## OUR URGE TO EXPLAIN
## CAN BECOME TOO STRONG

Deadline pressures on this book were used to justify a trip to a great spot overlooking a beach. Yesterday, Rachael and I drove through several fancy resorts a few miles from our more humble accommodations. I found myself lusting. How could I make enough money to come back next year and stay in one of those places?

Then I noticed my mind shifting in a more noble direction. Wouldn't it be great to bring our sons and their wives, to give them a vacation that right now they couldn't afford? But I couldn't afford an expensive vacation either. So I thought about this book I was writing. Could I sensationalize the topic and add a few heart-wrenching illustrations? Maybe then I could afford a wonderful family vacation. The beauty of the place would call us to worship. Maybe we'd even pray together on the beach.

I knew I was being sucked in, tempted to place money over message. And I began wondering why that fantasy was so compelling.

A distant memory came to mind. On the day before Christmas, when our kids were little, I'd look at their piles of gifts beneath the tree and worry that they might not be as excited as I wanted them to be the next morning. So I rushed out to the crowded mall to buy four or five more gifts for each of our sons.

I wondered if I was trying to reproduce in my children the happy feelings I felt as a kid at Christmas. Or maybe there was a void in me, something missing I wanted to give to my boys. These thoughts energized me. I liked exploring my thoughts, feelings, and motivations.

Then it dawned on me: I was searching for explanations. If I knew what was going on beneath my lust for luxury vacations, then perhaps I could manage it, control it, return to a more spiritual track in composing this book.

As my wife Rachael and I chatted about my thoughts, I said, somewhat sheepishly, "Maybe I should spend more energy in honoring how much I long to connect with our kids and with God as I write this book than figuring myself out." She thought that was a good idea. A phone call to each of our sons, praying with Rachael as we walked the beach together, and a time of studying the Bible proved far more valuable than obsessing about my motives.

Unexplained problems put us out of control. As a result, the urge to explain becomes stronger than the urge to connect, so strong that it may be getting in the way of developing deeper levels of trust.

## HUNTING FOR EXPLANATIONS

A friend told me he felt spiritually dead. A good sermon or some rousing worship times would lift him for a moment, but the deadness quickly returned. The Bible seemed dull, prayer was mere ritual, passion for God was gone. His strongest bursts of passion came when he read the newspaper's announcement that his favorite basketball team would play a televised game that week. But even that pleasure was fading. Beneath his activities, he couldn't shake a nagging sense of futility. He felt empty.

When a friend shares his struggles with me, the most natural thing in the world, especially since I am a psychologist, is to go hunting for explanations.

"You know, I used to have a problem with pornography," he offered. "It nearly destroyed our marriage when Debbie found out about it. But we're doing fine now. I've not gone back to the stuff since, and that's been over three years ago. Do you think I

30

still have unresolved guilt; or maybe the desire for pornography is still there, just repressed? I just can't figure out why I feel so dead all the time."

My friend was inviting me to join him on a Sherlock-Holmes-style investigation. I wonder what it would look like for him to invite me into a deeper connection where analysis would be relegated to a lesser place.

The urge to explain is strong. When a problem arises, we want to know what's wrong. And when we ask that question, a limited range of answers come to mind, answers that may lead us away from the joy that is available. We'll look at some of those answers in the next chapter.

# 3

# What Is Causing My Problem?

❦

OUR STRUGGLES COME IN two categories: Either we struggle to manage what can
be managed (like a stalled car or a warm
refrigerator); or we struggle, foolishly, to
manage what can never be managed (like an
angry wife or a sullen teenager).

In both cases, we try to figure out
what's behind our problems and what can
be done to improve things. In the first
category (call it Manageable Problems),
we're sometimes successful, like the mother
who enticed her children out of bed by heat-
ing their clothes, or like a friend who traced
his despondency to a chemical imbalance

and regained his zest for life through regular medication.

The second category (Unmanageable Problems) holds no success stories, not the "Here's what I did and look what happened" kind. Good things sometimes do occur (my stuttering stopped), but we're never exactly sure why. In this category, we're dealing with problems that can never be fully explained and therefore never fully controlled.

The fundamental problems of our existence, the problems that really matter, fall into this second category, problems like unhappiness, family breakups, suicide, loneliness, and rebellious kids. Most of the concerns we bring to friends, pastors, and counselors—uniquely human concerns—cannot be figured out and repaired. These problems exist because something is wrong with our lives that we can describe, discuss, and define, but never fully explain.

But we have made a terrible mistake. We have come to believe that most, if not all, of our problems are in the first category: Manageable Problems. We assume that our problems can be well enough understood to allow us to develop a comprehensive plan for tackling them that stands a reasonable chance for success. Most politicians, sociologists, and counselors direct their activities by this assumption. So do pastors, parents, and friends.

**The healing power of true connection sounds more like sentimental romance than hard-nosed reality.**

The idea that connection, that profound communion where life freely pours out of one person into the other and back again, could be really powerful in dealing with unmanageable problems, is hard to grasp. We're more drawn to explanation than to mystery, and we depend more on control than connection to solve our problems, even unmanageable ones. The healing power of true connection sounds more like sentimental romance than hard-nosed reality.

We really don't want to believe that any problem is unmanageable. Stubbornly, we assume that somewhere someone understands our problems, if not today, then certainly tomorrow; and that this understanding will make the solutions clear.

34

Christians take it a step further. We know God understands our problems, and he has been good enough to write a book explaining what we could not figure out on our own. Our job, we wrongly think, is to understand his explanations for the problems we experience and to then live according to whatever biblical principles apply to whatever we're doing. Doing what God says, in this way of thinking, has more to do with successfully managing our lives than with loving him. We approach God, not to know him, but to secure his cooperation in solving our problems.

We think like this about every aspect of our lives, but never more urgently than when we're facing a personal or relational problem. Let me illustrate.

## CHRIS AND SUSAN

Chris and Susan were sitting across the table from me. They were attending a conference at which I was speaking. On the second day, they requested time to meet with me. After a few minutes of get-acquainted conversation, Susan got things started.

"I know we don't have much time," she said. "Can I come right to the point? We really need your help. We've been married for seventeen years, and we just can't get close. And I don't know why. All I know is I'm terrified of him."

"I better clarify something," said her husband, Chris, smiling. "I don't beat my wife." Then, changing to the confident tone of a teacher, he said, "I know she worries about what I'm really thinking. I've never been one to wear my emotions on my sleeve, and that's hard for her. She comes from an Italian background, and I'm Dutch. She's probably too Italian, and I'm probably too Dutch. We saw a counselor for about a year who helped us recognize these patterns. It really did help."

"But you're still not close," I observed.

"No, but I think we're making head-way," Chris replied. "The counseling opened my eyes to our communication patterns. My wife can get pretty angry, and I don't see the hurt beneath it, so I react to the anger and get angry back or just retreat. I'm work-ing on responding to the pain she feels, and she's trying to let me see what's behind her anger."

"Your eyes dropped as Chris was talk-ing," I said to Susan. "How engaged did you feel with what he was saying?"

"Not very," Susan said, her eyes still

down. Then she looked up at me. "He makes it sound so simple. But it isn't." She paused. "There are other problems, too. Chris, tell him what you said to me last night about how mad you can get."

"For the past year or so, I've been worried about my anger," said Chris, thoughtful and subdued. "I don't understand what's happening. I've been yelling at drivers that irritate me more than I used to. I mean really yelling. Then, about six months ago, I began feeling anger toward our son, for nothing more than the normally irritating things four-year-old boys do. It's really scared me."

"It scares me, too," Susan said. "I can see it in his eyes. I don't think I'm worried that he'll ever hit me or abuse our son. It's more how he makes me feel, like I shouldn't even exist. I don't know why it gets to me so much, but it does. I don't want to be close to him. I'm too scared."

It's hard to listen to conversations like these without wondering "What's wrong?" without trying to understand the problem and figure out what could be done to remedy it. That, of course, is exactly what I want my dentist to do when I have a toothache. As I report my problem, I want him to figure out what's wrong. But that may not be the best direction for a counselor or friend to take when someone shares a personal problem.

But that's precisely what most counselors do. It's their job. Or so they think. And it's not only counselors. We all think that way. Problems kick our passion to explain into high gear.

Over the years, I've asked hundreds of counselees a standard question: "You've no doubt given a lot of thought to the problems you mention. What do you think might be going on?" After the usual "I really don't know" or "I have no idea," in every case a little prodding releases at least one suggested explanation. In twenty-five years of counseling, this question has never failed to evoke an answer. Problems drive all of us to ask what's wrong and to come up with a pet theory or two that gives us the illusion of being in full control of the solution.

When I asked Chris this question, he offered two possible explanations for his anger.

"About two years ago, Susan and I began talking about my quitting the insurance business to become full-time missionaries. It was right around then that my anger became a problem. I've wondered if it's an attack from Satan to make me feel unfit for missionary service. I've been reading up on spiritual warfare, and I think this really could be a battle with evil.

"But I've also wondered if my background might be involved. Maybe it's a psychological problem too. I mentioned that I'm Dutch. My father was a strict disciplinarian. He could be really harsh. He kept a strap on display in the kitchen that he used pretty freely, especially on me. Dad left Mother when I was sixteen for another woman he'd been seeing for years. I've seen him maybe a half dozen times since then. He sent a gift when our son was born. The counselor we saw commented on how matter-of-factly I described all this. He asked if I ever cried over all the pain with my dad. I never have. Maybe something is really blocked up inside me."

Chris was attempting to explain his problem. Once explained, perhaps something could be done.

When people reflect on their problems and ask what's wrong, the two categories Chris mentioned frequently come to mind— spiritual warfare and dysfunctional backgrounds. Other common categories include personal sin, biochemical disorder, undisciplined living, and deficient spirituality.

Let's briefly consider each one.

## Spiritual Warfare

My wife, Rachael, occasionally experiences night terrors. Without warning, she'll suddenly sit up in bed at two A.M., look around our bedroom with an expression of sheer horror on her face, and sometimes break into frenzied sobbing.

A sleep disorders clinic Rachael went to observed unusual muscular activity while she slept. When she takes the medication they prescribed, she experiences no episodes of the terror but wakes up groggy and unrested. Is her problem medical? Are drugs our best answer?

After eighteen years of marriage (and I say all of this with her explicit permission), she confided in me that as a child she had been sexually abused over a period of several years. We talked about it extensively. She also shared this information with several wise godly women whom she trusts; they have prayed and counseled with her.

We've wondered if spiritual warfare plays a part in her ongoing sleep problem. Perhaps the devil gained a foothold in her life through the abuse, and the remedy is deliverance. We've prayed, claimed authority over Satan, gone through several lists of steps recommended by leaders in the spiritual warfare movement (lists that center mostly on renouncing footholds), and we've even played hymns softly in the background as we've slept. So far the hymns seem to help the most.

Rachael and I believe there is a devil who commands an army of corrupted angels. We further believe that we're in a battle against these spiritual forces and that our only hope is the full armor of God. But we've observed that those who write extensively about these matters tend to come up with a system, an explanation of the warfare that reduces our battle to a specific procedure. I worry that, once we have a system, we're in danger of placing more faith in a manageable plan with predictable results than in God, who is neither manageable nor predictable.

If playing hymns (or anything else) becomes our battle plan, then when it doesn't work, when our explanation fails, we buy another book in search of a better explanation; we look for a more effective plan.

## Dysfunctional Background

In our psychologized culture, our thoughts naturally gravitate toward a psychological explanation behind our personal struggles. These explanations usually include a difficult history of trauma or neglect that presumably damaged our emotional development. The path to recovery involves overcoming denial of all that was painful and "working through" its continuing effects. Evidence of damage to our psyche includes such things as self-hatred, low self-esteem, irrational fears, and unprovoked rage, as well as a wide range of other psychological symptoms.

> *Our hope may lie not in managing our problems, but in connecting with good people.*

Counselors are fond of saying things like, "As I listen to you describe your concern, I hear many signs that point to a history of sexual abuse," or "Your fear of your husband makes me wonder if you learned to fear men when you were a little girl." And the search for an explanation begins.

Many therapists would, I think, follow Chris's lead and explore the effects of his father's harshness and eventual desertion on

Chris's sense of self-worth. After teaching counseling for fourteen years, I've noticed that many beginning counselors (and more than a few veterans) assume that great progress is being made when a counselee "gets in touch" with long buried feelings. If Chris were to break down as he verbally relived his difficult childhood, his tears would likely be hailed as a major breakthrough on his road to recovery.

Please hear me carefully. I am not suggesting that these ideas are necessarily wrong. Difficult backgrounds do leave deep wounds. Finally feeling long-suppressed pain can represent a breakthrough.

Instead, I am suggesting that we often build these ideas into a system that satisfies our desire for explanation and leads to a prescribed course of treatment, a course that often depends on the insights of a skilled counselor. I am suggesting that we may have the resources for dealing with our struggles right at our fingertips, that our hope may lie not in managing our problems, but in connecting with good people.

## Personal Sin

Another popular explanation for behavioral and emotional problems, especially among more conservative Christians, is personal sin. This explanation comes complete with a "treatment plan," consisting of conviction, confession, repentance, and obedience. The sin may be obvious, like having an affair, or it may be subtle, like a self-centered concern for gaining approval from people rather than giving to them.

In previous books, I described the subtle sin of self-protection. Anything we do, no matter how apparently innocent or good, that is motivated by protecting ourselves against personal pain and that displays insensitivity to the needs of someone else is sin. It is a violation of love. If a husband kisses his wife to prevent her from asking embarrassing questions when he arrives home late, the kiss is sin.

Personal sin may be consciously chosen, like telling a lie, or it may involve behaviors over which the individual seemingly has no control, like sexual addiction. Some Christians insist that whether the sin feels chosen or not, it's still sin and responsibility is equal in either case. Others agree, but are willing to explore unnoticed sin that could lie behind the compulsive behavior.

I remember a seminary student taking

a counselor to task for wanting to explore what might lie behind the student's admitted struggle with compulsive masturbation. With great indignation, he scolded the counselor for using a "psychological" approach. "You should have called it sin and exhorted me to stop it, then held me accountable to do so. That's biblical counseling." But biblical counseling, I would argue, includes connecting with people through entering into the thoughts and intents of the heart that lie behind visible sin.

## Biochemical Disorder

With modern advances in medicine, the theory that many (if not all) personal struggles have a physical basis continues to spread. Mood swings, depression, anxiety attacks, obsessive-compulsive disorders, psychotic thought patterns—all are believed to reflect a biochemical disorder.

Often, psychiatrists practice very little psychotherapy and indeed receive minimal training in psychotherapy during their residency. Instead, they rely exclusively on treating their patients with "psychoactive" drugs. The issue, of course, is whether the problem is caused by a physical illness that can be medically treated. If so, it makes no sense to waste time talking about one's feelings or difficult backgrounds. Get on with the real treatment of restoring chemical balance to a disordered physical system.

I have no quarrel with diagnosing some problems as physically caused and treating them accordingly. But it is important to recognize how an explanation-hungry society wants to believe that most problems have a medical origin. Not only can a biochemical diagnosis explain a problem, it also provides a scientific basis for controlling it. Once again, the power of community, where people connect with people, is not needed; expertise will do the job.

## Undisciplined Living

A good friend reacted to his wife's declaration that she didn't love him by vowing to become a better person. He gave up drinking, scheduled more time at home, went on a diet, and began a program to read through the Bible in one year. As he explained to me, "Things fall into place when you live responsibly."

Few of us have trouble identifying pockets of sloppy living. When a relationship breaks down or our pressured lives show signs of coming apart, we are tempted to indict undisciplined living as the culprit. The cure then is obvious: more exercise, more acts of kindness, more church committee assignments, less television, fewer desserts, less spending; in other words, more of what we don't want and less of what we do want. Even if it costs us pleasure, we love explaining our problems in ways that allow us to do something about them. And that's the problem. When we explain our difficulties as caused by undisciplined living, we're back in the saddle again, fully in control, riding through life with no felt need for a guide to lead us over unfamiliar terrain.

## Deficient Spirituality

Our culture is in the midst of a spiritual awakening, a renewed interest in finding satisfaction in something other than things and pleasure and achievement.

More and more people are explaining their problems as evidence of deep emptiness and a sense of futility. They, therefore, seek a richer experience of spirituality.

If nothing else, this trend aims people toward the mysterious and away from control. But even here the demand for a system rears its ugly head. We organize this search for meaning into something we can manage, into a procedure with predictable results. Meditation exercises, silent retreats, and contemplative prayer can be reduced to formulas for connecting with God rather than treated as opportunities for God to break through into our lives any way he chooses. Deficient spirituality sometimes provides only one more explanation for our struggles, one more way of helping us manage our lives.

## WHAT'S WRONG?

What's wrong with our lives? It's a question we all ask. The answer we give determines who we think can help us. Does Chris, the angry husband, need a therapist, a pastor, or a good friend? Maybe he needs to assume more responsibility for his life. Or perhaps he just needs more of God? Or maybe some medication?

What does he need? What do any of us need when we struggle? And who can help? That's the question we ask in Part 2.

# PART 2

# Who Can Help?

# 4

# Four Resources
# I Can Draw From

⁂

**W**HEN PEOPLE FIND THEMSELVES struggling, the first question they ask is, "What's wrong?" In Part 1 of this book, after considering why that question is so important to us, we suggested that the answers people come up with fall into six categories of explanation. The next four chapters take up the second question, "Who can help?" Let me summarize what we've already said and anticipate where we're going.

## QUESTION #1: WHAT'S WRONG?
Six categories of explanation for personal struggles

1. SPIRITUAL WARFARE: The cause is **demonic**.
2. DYSFUNCTIONAL BACK-GROUND: The cause is **psychological.**
3. PERSONAL SIN: The cause is **moral.**
4. BIOCHEMICAL DISORDER: The cause is **medical.**
5. UNDISCIPLINED LIVING: The cause is **weakness.**
6. DEFICIENT SPIRITUALITY: The cause is **distance from God.**

# QUESTION #2: WHO CAN HELP?
Four resources that I may need to draw from

1. THE INDIVIDUAL: Responsibility for change falls largely on my shoulders.
2. NATURAL COMMUNITY: Support from family, friends, and pastors might be useful.
3. GOD: I must tap into God's sufficient power. He is all I need.
4. PROFESSIONAL HELP: Trained specialists may be necessary.

The four chapters of Part 2 discuss these four resources. Keep one simple thought in mind as you read: the way we explain our problems (how we answer the first question) determines who we depend on for help (the answer to the second).

Let's take a look at what happens when we turn to the first resource, when we depend primarily on ourselves to fight through our struggles.

# 5

# I Must Help Myself

❦

I REMEMBER SITTING in Sunday school class feeling very confused. I was eight years old. My buddy Jimmy, the other member of our two-boy class, was paying close attention to the lesson. I figured I was the only one, probably in the whole world, who didn't get it.

Mr. Van Buchwold had positioned two cloth dogs on the flannelgraph board. One was black, the other white. He explained that these two dogs were living in our hearts. The black one (our old nature) made us want to do bad things. The white one (our new nature) prompted us in good directions. "Whenever you know what you should do but are tempted to do something else, those two dogs are fighting inside you. Whichever one you say 'sic 'em' to will win. It's up to you."

That week in school I had a spelling test. I was a good speller. I had won every spelling bee that Miss Webster, our third-grade teacher, had held. Except one. That was last week, when I missed a word—and Lyle spelled it correctly. Now we were taking this week's test. Suddenly I stiffened. I wasn't sure how to spell the last word Miss Webster had called out.

> The Bible tells us to put to death our lusts and evil desires. But how do we do that?

Lyle was sitting to my right, a little ahead. If I lifted my head and tilted it to a certain angle, I would be able to see how he had spelled that difficult word.

Then I remembered last Sunday's lesson. I could almost hear the dogs barking. I made a decision to do the right thing, which to me meant turning loose the good dog. But I wasn't exactly sure how to do it. I remember visualizing both animals snarling at each other and, turning my mind to the white one, muttering, "Sic 'em" under my breath.

Then I sat there, for maybe two seconds. Nothing happened. The urge to cheat remained strong. I wanted to be the spelling king. So I lifted my head to the necessary angle, copied Lyle's version on my paper, and waited for Miss Webster to announce the next word.

When trouble came, I didn't ask for anyone's help in resisting temptation. I figured it was up to me. I may have shot up a quick prayer to God, but the decision was mine. I was on my own, battling competing urges within me as best I could. But I couldn't get the victory.

As other problems have come my way, I've often felt alone and powerless in my struggles. I suspect a lot of other people have, too. Perhaps many have shared the confusion I first felt looking at those two dogs when I was eight years old.

The confusion is real. The Bible tells us to put to death our lusts and evil desires (Col. 3:5). But how do we do that? Surely there must be more to it than saying "sic 'em" to our nobler thoughts.

# AN ONGOING STRUGGLE

A missionary once told me that, when he was ten, his sixteen-year-old brother began a pornography distribution business in their neighborhood, and he was conscripted to be the delivery boy. He remembers loading the magazines and calendars in his little red wagon and rolling them to the meeting points agreed upon with the buyers. During the two years that the business prospered, before it was discovered and shut down, he had seen more pornographic pictures than most people see in a lifetime.

The pornography left its mark. The bad dog inside his heart had grown big and strong. And becoming a Christian during college years had not seemed to kill it. Now, as a career missionary with a wonderful wife and three kids he adored, he continued to struggle with his addiction to pornography.

"I just can't get permanent victory," he told me. "Sometimes it's only the images in my mind I can't get rid of. Other times I've looked at the stuff in convenience stores. Occasionally, I've actually bought one of those awful magazines. Then I get so disgusted I throw it away and promise myself and God I'll never do it again. But I always do. The desires are still there."

What does it mean for him to "put to death sexual impurity, lust, and evil desires"?

He went on. "I once saw a counselor. He said he was a Christian. When I told him about my introduction to pornography at age ten, he wanted to spend a lot of time talking about that. He asked about my relationship with my brother, then and now, as well as how I got along with my parents. I only went to him twice. I know we're victims of our past. If my brother had never run a pornography business, I'd probably not be struggling like I am today.

"But I chose to look at those magazines then, and I'm choosing to do it today. I have no one to blame but myself. And it's my job to stay in the Word enough and to depend on Christ living in me so that I don't yield to the flesh."

This man explained his struggle as the product of personal sin and undisciplined living. He was making bad choices and was not consistent enough in good habits, like Bible reading and prayer. By accepting these two categories of explanation, he concluded that change was his responsibility. God had already done his part: he had provided forgiveness, an indwelling Spirit, clear instructions, and access to the throne. The rest was up to him. They were his choices to make. Neither friend nor pastor could make his decisions for him. And asking a therapist to treat a sexual addiction seemed to him a cop-out. To his way of thinking, the necessary resources needed to change were already inside of him.

Many people answer the question "Who can help?" with the answer: "It's up to me. God has already given me what I need to make the right choices." And this answer is difficult to challenge without appearing to contradict essential Christian truths. When I suggested to one man that he might profit from talking through some issues in his life with a wise counselor, he immediately retorted, "I don't buy all that psychological mumbo jumbo about deep-seated emotional problems. All you shrinks end up doing is blaming everybody but the guy who's choosing to mess up his life with wrong choices."

But those who place all the burden for change on themselves, who assume that personal struggles are best handled by assuming responsibility for right choices, often stumble into one of two consequences. They become either blind or frustrated.

# Blindness

People who believe they must handle all their problems on their own often refuse to face problems they can't handle. Blinders are fixed firmly in place to narrow awareness of what is happening within their hearts and in their relationships. The effect is a smug satisfaction that they are managing their lives quite well, an impression shared by no one who knows them.

I am sometimes taken aback by how blinding the blinders can be. Many years ago, my wife and I were guests in the home of a young pastor. Before dinner, we were socializing in the living room with the cleric and his wife, a frail-looking, nervous woman who always seemed ready to jump up and do something. Their two small children were playing quietly in the adjoining family room, in clear range of their father's frequent stare. They seemed more well-behaved than happy.

At one point, with all the charm of a drill sergeant, the pastor turned to his wife and barked, "I want a cup of coffee." I immediately understood why she had seemed so ready to jump. She scurried off to the kitchen, much like a dog would run after a bone it was ordered to fetch.

The pastor then turned back to me (not to my wife) and uttered one of the most annoying sentences I have ever heard: "I really don't want a cup of coffee, but it's good to remind her who's the head of this house." He was utterly oblivious to his cruelty, to his wife's insulted dignity, and to how badly my wife and I wished she would return from the kitchen and pour the cup of coffee on his head.

Had he recognized either his own tyranny or his wife's deep hatred of herself (and probably him), he would not, I suspect, have had the foggiest notion how to respond. When people face only those parts of life that allow them to maintain the illusion of control, they eventually lose touch with the rich human elements, both noble and wicked, that make up our existence.

**People who believe they must handle all their problems on their own often refuse to face problems they can't handle.**

## Frustration

Kinder people who explain their problems in terms of personal sin and undisciplined living tend to become more frustrated than blind, frustrated both with the shallowness of their relationships and with their inability to measure up to the high standards they set for themselves. For them, "carrying your own load" (Paul's admonition in Galatians 6:5) means fully unburdening yourself to no one, and "walking in the truth" (2 John 3:4) allows no room for significant failure. The first idea keeps relationships distant; the second creates intolerable pressure.

> It's hard to believe that anyone cares. It's even harder to believe that anyone could help.

When the center of life is reduced to living better and more responsibly, our hearts scream for a level of fellowship we do not know and for a joy we can only imagine. Unless, of course, the determination to manage life hardens us to the unmanageable parts;

62

then our screaming frustration yields to the contentment of blindness.

But the integrity of many folks won't allow a blindness to develop that relieves their frustration. So they continue on, doing their best to stay on diets, to resist urges to buy pornography, to read their Bibles more consistently, and to overcome the desire to go back to bed and never get up. On some days it seems like a losing battle. Then on others, victory comes closer, and they're encouraged. Till the next setback.

It's hard to believe that anyone cares. It's even harder to believe that anyone could help. Prayer, words of encouragement, pats on the back, sharing similar struggles, even a richer understanding of the struggles— nothing can help but making good choices if our problems can all be traced back to personal sin and undisciplined living.

That's the position Milt has taken. He feels the frustration but doesn't see any path away from it. Four years ago, he was invited to leave the large church he had successfully pastored for fifteen years to assume a leadership role at denominational headquarters. The committee implied that they wanted to groom him for senior leadership, perhaps to succeed the current elderly president. After months of prayer, Milt agreed to come.

He felt privileged to work so closely with the revered old gentleman. Like nearly everyone in their fellowship, he stood in awe of the white-haired saint with the piercing eyes and quiet voice. It took a month for Milt to see what only a few close associates had known for years and kept to themselves. Behind the scenes, the president was a rigid tyrant who controlled denominational business with an iron, self-serving hand. Milt made the mistake of not keeping the observation to himself. He raised questions at the executive board meeting. Within a week, he was asked to resign.

That happened a little more than three years ago. Since then, Milt has not found any position within the church fellowship, neither in administration nor pastoral work. He has always believed life could be unfair. Now he had personal experience of that fact. He battled with depression, cynicism, anxiety, and the urge for revenge.

But he believed that the real battle was always against personal sin. His job was to yank out the logs in his own eyes and to let God deal with the splinters in everyone else's, even if those splinters looked to him like the trunk of a California redwood.

Once, when Milt felt suicidal, he considered seeing a psychologist. But instead, he got on his knees and prayed. Then he found a secular job and decided with his wife to sponsor the junior high youth group at a church they had been attending, a church outside the fellowship.

I am Milt's friend. He told me his story after he heard me publicly share that I was going through a battle with a loss of confidence in my abilities. Over lunch, he said that he wasn't sure he could ever teach or preach effectively again. When I probed a bit, the whole story came out. He concluded our time together by saying, "I just need to keep believing that God is good and keep my nose clean." Then he added, "But it's really hard. I feel so frustrated."

Frustration affects many people who try hard to change. Sometimes even these independent folks do what many of us do when we hurt: they seek help from their peers. And that's our topic in the next chapter.

**Frustration affects many people who try hard to change.**

# 6

# Maybe Other People Could Help

⁓◇◇⁓

MY FRIEND DAVID has an awful marriage. No screaming fights, no threats of divorce. Just coldness; lonely, distant coldness. I asked him when he last enjoyed an affectionate hug with his wife. He answered, "It's been a long time."

Recently, David was passed over for an expected job promotion, a move up that carried with it enough of a salary increase to make college bills almost manageable.

I asked him how he was handling it, both his dead marriage and the denied promotion. "I just don't think about it much. I go to work, pay whatever bills I can, and try to stay civil with my wife. What else can I do?" He paused, then added, "But it does feel good to talk about it with you. I know you can't make anything better for me, but it feels good to just say it out loud. I guess I could use some encouragement. Thanks for listening."

That's how most of us feel: encouragement doesn't do much good, but still we like it. Of course we have to struggle with our problems as best we can, but a listening ear, a supportive comment, a caring heart touches an ache within that continuing on responsibly doesn't quite relieve. We value the encouragement that occurs when something uniquely human comes out of another person and into us.

But that kind of encouragement doesn't happen often. We're more accustomed to a milder variety, some pleasant words, a piece of friendly advice, an ear that almost listens, a hang-in-there slap on the back.

Why? Why is deep encouragement rare? We're with people every day, good people, kind people, people who really do care. Why are moments of rich encouragement so infrequent? Let me suggest three reasons.

# REASON #1: A WRONG ASSUMPTION

Part of the problem is our assumption that real help for real problems requires the services of an expert. We assume wrongly that friends and family, even pastors, can't do very much. We have learned to undervalue the encouragement of ordinary people. Like a poor person with a friend who is deeply in debt, we don't believe we have much to offer. There's nothing much we can do.

At some level, we know better. We know the profound impact that true compassion has made on our lives. We know what it means to share an ugly secret with a friend who doesn't judge us or back away. Even folks who report that they were greatly helped by a professional counselor often look back on their sessions with more appreciation for their counselor's concern and involvement than for his special skill. When people tell the stories of their journey, the life-changing events that stand out are often simple experiences of somebody's care. That should tell us something.

When our family first moved to Warsaw, a small town in Indiana, we immediately plunged into the responsibilities of settling in. We unpacked boxes, opened a new checking account, and stocked our new refrigerator. It felt good to get things done.

But not as good as we wanted to feel. I remember driving along Center Street looking for a hardware store saying to myself, "I don't belong here. I can't even find a place to buy a staple gun. And I don't have one friend I can call for help. No one knows I'm here, and no one cares. This isn't home."

I eventually found the store and made my purchase. When I returned home, my two sons were playing tennis with each other at the neighborhood courts and my wife was on her knees tearing into the next box. As I walked in the back door, the phone rang—the first call on our newly installed phone.

It was Becky, Mike's wife, someone we had met recently at a seminar and instantly

*Part of the problem is our assumption that real help for real problems requires the services of an expert.*

69

liked. "Mike and I wondered if you'd want to meet us downtown at a diner that serves a great Greek salad. It's just across from the courthouse on the east side. Will that work?"

Will it work? A call informing me I had just won the lottery would not have been more welcome. We showered, changed, stopped by the tennis courts to tell our kids where we were going, and drove into town.

Three hours later, after four pretty good Greek salads, one vanilla malted, about eight cups of coffee, and three pieces of freshly baked cherry pie, Rachael and I drove home encouraged. Our time with Mike and Becky put a whole new frame around the picture of our new life in the Midwest. Warsaw suddenly seemed like a nice place to live, a friendly town with convenient hardware stores and pleasant tellers at the bank. We felt hope, a hope provided by nothing more than a moment of connection with good folks. And that connection meant the world to us.

But maybe that's making too much out of an "isn't that nice?" kind of story. Truth is, our problems weren't very big. We were a happy family moving into a comfortable home who were feeling the predictable and temporary loneliness that relocation always brings. For problems like that—small, symptomatic of nothing serious—encouragement is wonderful.

But what happens when your daughter has lost twenty pounds, and you're terrified she's anorexic? What about the loneliness of widowhood or the shame of sexual perversion? What role does encouragement play when we face real problems?

For many people, the answer is well expressed in two words:

> What role does encouragement play when we face real problems?

Not much! Even when encouragement comes, it doesn't have the power to address big problems. We need expert help, help from people who have been specially trained to tackle serious concerns. That's the assumption we make.

## REASON #2: TURNING TO THE WRONG PERSON

The second reason that encouragement often falls short is that we turn, unknowingly, to the wrong people for help.

Shirley lost her husband to another woman. At the same time her teenage daughter announced she was pregnant. The divorce left her with neither the funds she needed to pay the bills nor the emotional support to cope with her daughter's pregnancy. She felt alone, desperate, confused, cheated—and vulnerable.

The elders at her church had prayed for her. Ron, one of the elders who was known for his compassion, paid Shirley a visit to encourage her. He was a widower and a successful businessman with plenty of money. The visit led to a warm greeting the next Sunday, then to lunch after church, and then to dinner at his country club.

Several women friends who knew Ron warned her to be careful. He had a reputation for being a bit weird. Shirley understood—and shared—their concerns. But within four months, she married him.

Within two weeks of their wedding, Ron began insisting that Shirley keep receipts for every dime she spent, that she account for every minute of her day in a written diary, and that she greet him every evening in a provocative dress.

Shirley didn't know what to do. Efforts to communicate her concerns incensed him and only intensified his suspicion and demands. Not knowing where else to turn, she confided in a friend, a woman she had known for years. Her friend told her to move out and file for divorce and seemed irritated when Shirley expressed hesitation about doing so.

She told another friend. This one said, "I warned you he was weird," then added, "I have no idea what you should do. Maybe you ought to talk with our pastor."

Shirley's meeting with the pastor was a disaster. After sharing a little bit of her story, the pastor firmly instructed her to cooperate with her husband and assured her that Ron wasn't as bad as she thought. If she were submissive, he would treat her right.

She stopped going to church, sought help from a private Christian counselor, felt heard, and found the strength to remain kind to Ron without yielding to his inappropriate demands. Eventually Ron falsely accused her of adultery and, with the church's blessing, filed for divorce.

When Shirley first heard me teach in a seminar that the church should be a good place to turn to find help with personal struggles, she almost jumped to her feet and shouted, "NO!"

We're appropriately outraged by stories

in which hurting folks turn to people whom they think can help only to be hurt more as a result.

## REASON #3: ENCOURAGEMENT IS OFTEN FEEBLE

Most of us have learned to settle for the only encouragement we've ever received without wondering if perhaps it is a weak, shallow counterfeit of what God intends. Perhaps the encouragement we know is weak, but maybe there's a stronger variety.

We want there to be. We want to talk with our friends and find real help for real problems. But our experience weakens our hope. Maybe encouragement is no more helpful than a friendly dog licking our face when it sees us cry. A friend's kind words and a dog's warm lick are both nice gestures, and we're appreciative. They do make us feel better. But

> We assume that we can't get help from our friends, simply because they are not professionals.

neither really helps. So we pat the dog on the head and leave our family and friends in search of the help we need.

Katie worked up her nerve to make known a burden to Millicent, her prayer partner. "I'm just so worried about Mark. He's sixteen now and getting really disrespectful, mostly to me. I asked Peter to step in more firmly and deal with Mark, but he won't do it. He thinks I'm blowing this out of proportion. I feel so unprotected by my husband and hated by my son."

Millicent replied, "Every family has troubles. I'm really sorry you're going through all this. It's probably just a stage for Mark, and Peter is such a good guy. I hope you hang in there till it all gets better."

At best, that's feeble encouragement.

## MERE ENCOURAGEMENT

As a culture, we assume that the resources of community, particularly church community, are suitable to help with small problems, but big ones require the services of someone qualified to expertly deal with our difficulties. It is a serious mistake—so we think—to expect the input of friends and pastors to do for us what only stronger forms of help can provide. We assume that we can't get help from our friends, simply because they are not professionals.

People who hurt often try to make it on their own. If that effort fails, they sometimes turn to others for encouragement. If what they receive is either pleasant but weak, like a dog's friendly lick, or insensitive and damaging, they may decide that only God can supply the help they need. The next chapter explores what may happen when hurting people directly pursue God for help.

# 7

# Only God Can Help

⌒❧⌒

As our culture continues its love affair with technology, its confidence in human achievement buoyed by medical breakthroughs and computer miracles, a different passion is emerging. People are paying more attention to the spiritual side of life. We are more willing to "explain" certain phenomena as evidence of an unseen spirit world. Belief in angels is no longer found only among conservative Christians and delusional mental patients. It's no longer just preachers or black musicians who speak of the soul. Prominent psychotherapists are becoming spiritual directors. Books on caring for the soul are coming out of general publishing houses.

All of this emboldens Christians to suspect what they've wondered all along: maybe Frank Peretti was not writing fiction in *This Present Darkness*. Maybe a lot of our problems are the visible fallout of an invisible war being waged between supernatural forces of evil and supernatural forces of good. Perhaps the real problem is spiritual warfare.

But there is another possibility. Some folks are not inclined to interpret problems as demonically inspired but still think of them as essentially spiritual. Increasing numbers of people, both in the church and outside of it, are attributing their difficulties to deficient spirituality, to a character structure not sufficiently energized by connection with God.

Spiritual warfare and deficient spirituality have become more common as "explanations" for our problems. In both, people are driven to set their minds on things above, to see what cannot be seen, to more deeply experience the power and presence of God.

Some folks turn to New Age ideas. Others are drawn to eastern mysticism. More than a few Christians are leaving evangelical churches for congregations with more liturgy. Some prefer freer expressions of worship that encourage more dramatic experiences as they participate.

Most conservative Christians who are eager for richer experiences of God begin to take their faith more seriously, to expect an encounter with the supernatural, and to look more carefully within themselves for obstacles to knowing Christ.

But that worthy beginning sometimes takes a wrong turn and leaves people more frustrated and disillusioned than radiant and believing. Two common problems that people often attribute to spiritual sources will help me make my point: obsessive thoughts and self-hatred.

> *Spiritual warfare and deficient spirituality have become more common as "explanations" for our problems.*

## OBSESSIVE THOUGHTS
Graduate school prepared me well for handling cases that comfortably fit within the

theories I had studied. I felt relieved, for example, when a client presented a phobic reaction to something specific—like a fear of flying—because I had a tidy explanation for his symptom and a clear-cut procedure for helping him.

But too often, I was asked to treat problems that I couldn't squeeze into my theories and that wouldn't yield to my assortment of therapeutic tricks. Obsessive symptoms fell into that category. Otherwise normal, well-adjusted people would complain of abnormal thoughts and urges that would intrude unbidden into their consciousness and sometimes plague their every waking minute.

I remember one seminary student who could not stop worrying over his last sin. When I first counseled him, his last "sin" was raising his hand to ask a question during a classroom lecture. The professor made no effort to conceal his irritation with the uninvited interruption.

The student felt awful, as if he had committed an unpardonable offense. For the next several weeks, he experienced a strong urge to apologize to the professor every time he passed him in the hallway. In conversation with me, he was quick to admit that his "sin" was entirely appropriate behavior and, if anything was really sinful, it was the professor's irritability.

But that realization didn't help. The urge to think about his sin remained strong. Relief from his painful sense of guilt came only when he apologized. The relief, however, lasted maybe five minutes, then the guilt returned with greater strength.

Most psychologists would have little trouble explaining this student's obsession in familiar categories—unresolved guilt from significant failure (perhaps forgotten), the legacy from overly strict parents of an overactive conscience, or deep insecurity that only universal acceptance could satisfy. But, as every therapist knows, insight into the dynamics of a symptom doesn't always get rid of it.

Psychiatrists theorize that obsessions may have an organic cause. Many report success in treating them with medication. But the nature of obsessive thoughts raises an interesting question. Most uncontrollable thoughts drive their victims in morally or at least socially bad or distorted directions. Why don't people struggle with overwhelming urges to do good? If the cause is found in morally neutral chemical imbalances or neurological disorders, one might expect that the resultant obsessions would divide evenly between good ones and bad ones.

But people who struggle with obsessive thoughts (and their numbers are greater than many think) want to jump from high places, push others down long flights of stairs, act crazily in dignified situations, and engage in immoral, often violent, sexual activity. Obscene words and blasphemous ideas take up residence in their minds and will not leave. The question must be asked: Is it possible that such thoughts and urges have their source in supernatural evil?

Spiritual warfare is now widely believed to be at the root of many cases of depression, anxiety, and sexual perversions, as well as obsessive thoughts and

> No sooner do we get into the fight than we insist on organizing our strategy. We soon depend more on the battle plan than on the power behind it.

compulsive disorders. The result is that people are abandoning more traditional forms of treatment like therapy or medication and joining the battle against evil principalities.

Agreeing with Paul that our battle is against principalities and powers is a good beginning. But the first wrong turn is taken quickly. No sooner do we get into the fight than we insist on organizing our strategy. We soon depend more on the battle plan than on the power behind it. Let me explain.

In his important book *The Trivialization of God*, author Don McCullough argues that God is trivialized whenever we enlist his support to aid our causes. He points out how easy it is to mistake our agenda for God's, to think we're following him when, in fact, we're insisting that he follow us.

**One sure sign that we're trivializing God is that we provide him with a job description that we expect him to perform on command.**

But, even when we offer him a five-star rank, God is not easily conscripted into our army to wage war against enemy activity that we think he must hate as much as we do. We have a hard time imagining a good agenda that includes temporary suffering from any cause, especially from spiritual forces, and therefore assume that God is always on the side of less struggle.

One sure sign that we're trivializing God is that we provide him with a job description that we expect him to perform on command. We organize our tactics according to a theology that says we can reliably harness God's power through specific activity on our part. We create lists of spiritual disciplines to follow and write manuals on how to practice them properly; we compose carefully worded prayers to recite; we learn to pronounce victory over the devil in formula-like fashion. We stick close to our formulas believing that if we veer from them we might not be as effective.

I remember a particularly strange episode in my life. I was teaching a three-week summer course at a southern Bible college and living with my family in campus housing. One especially hot night I couldn't sleep. The open bedroom window in our non-air-

84

conditioned apartment was only letting in more muggy air.

Suddenly, a violent image entered my mind, something thoroughly distasteful to me that fascinated me as much as it disgusted me. I couldn't stop thinking about it. And then, lying there in the quiet darkness, an eerie sense came over me that I was in the presence of evil. I began to perspire from more than the heat.

I sat up in bed. Speaking softly so as not to wake my wife, I claimed the power of Jesus' blood as my protection from whatever or whoever was in the room. I recited Bible verses about the power in me that was greater than the power in the world and, with a firm spirit that I hoped disguised my terror, reminded Satan that he was a defeated foe.

But what stands out more clearly in my memory of that night is interesting: I kept wondering if I was doing it right. I felt like the little boy holding the magic lantern, trying to remember if I was supposed to rub it two times or three. I wasn't believing in a God whose power was already at work. Instead, I was trusting in the correctness of my own efforts to coax God to give me what I wanted.

Imagine Moses worrying about holding

his staff at a certain angle to make certain that the wall of water didn't collapse too soon. We trivialize God when we depend more on the precision of our tactics than on his loving heart. When we explain problems like obsessive thoughts as evidence of spiritual warfare, we may enter the right battle but quickly turn in the wrong direction of too much organization. The result, even when we are asking for more of God, is frustration, and sometimes the end of hope.

## SELF-HATRED

Those who have not struggled with intense self-hatred cannot know how crippling a problem it can be—or how stubborn. It begins with a moment of self-doubt, perhaps triggered by a small failure, a minor snub, or demeaning words. The sense that we are worthy of neglect, that nothing in us should be liked or taken seriously, passes quickly, but the question has been raised.

Years pass. We experience more failure, failure with enduring consequences, like losing a job or discouraging our children or severely hurting a spouse. And we're failed by others. Friends betray us. Good relationships disintegrate. Unkind words, some mean-spirited and vicious, reach our ears and lodge in our hearts. At first we're angry, maybe self-righteous: "He was so wrong to treat me that way." Then we wonder—maybe it's our fault.

Given enough time and misfortune, we reach a fateful decision: We're bad, not in the moral sense of sinful, but rather in the shameful sense of lacking value. We're stupid or fat or weak or perverted or overbearing or nerdy. Something is wrong with who we are that we can't do anything about.

Every conversation and social encounter confirms our fear: We are bad. No one wants to sit with us at church. Our husband doesn't laugh at a joke we tell. The pastor greets the person in front of us long enough to not have to greet us.

People who struggle with this level of self-hatred know that becoming more responsible doesn't help. Clean garages and balanced checkbooks generate some satisfaction, but the contempt they have for themselves is not dislodged. Nothing helps.

Something about self-hatred makes it difficult for the struggling individual to share it with his physician. It's embarrassing. And besides, all the doctor can prescribe is mood-altering drugs. Drugs may generate energy, even a bit of cheer, but the conviction of self-hatred is not weakened through medication.

*Those who have not struggled with intense self-hatred cannot know how crippling a problem it can be.*

Spiritual warfare may be a possibility, but self-hating people are more likely to explain their disdain for themselves as a legitimate response to their badly flawed character. They hear stories of God working in other people's lives—and feel discouraged. "It'll never happen to me. I'm just not godly enough." They explain their problem as deficient spirituality.

If the explanation for the problem is deficient spirituality, then the solution must be improved spirituality, which sometimes takes the form of seeking God in hopes of experiencing his transforming power and presence.

But that effort can easily lead to over-organization of our spiritual life, the first wrong turn. We may outline a step-by-step procedure to find God. We may set the stage for God to come to us in transforming power by fasting or spending more time in Bible study and prayer. Or we may take a second wrong turn by just remaining faithful and passively waiting, hoping that God will meet us in a mystical experience.

We know we can't manipulate God into appearing on demand, so we either keep on hoping that something supernatural will happen, or, when nothing happens, we give up in despair.

## WHAT NEXT?

We know only God can help. We're dealing with our sin as best we can; we've committed ourselves to living responsibly; we're open to explaining our problems as the result of physical illness that God might treat through medicine; we've joined the battle against evil powers, hoping we're using the proper weapons in the right way; and we're seeking God, wanting to know him in a way that transforms our lives.

Many apparently sincere seekers of God are still frustrated. There's got to be more help, they conclude, another avenue to walk down that will lead to a happier, less problem-filled life. Maybe it's time to consider professional help. Maybe it's time to see a counselor.

# 8

# Maybe I Need Professional Help

⌒∞⌒

AFTER WATCHING HER HUSBAND become more and more discouraged with his work and isolated from her family, Marti finally worked up the courage to say, "I think you're suffering from depression. I don't know if you need medication or therapy, but I really think you need professional help."

The suggestion frightened Tom. He had felt alone for years, shut up in the cave of worries and struggles he had shared with no one. The idea of opening up to another human being terrified him. But, he thought, maybe talking to a professional, someone he didn't know, in a confidential relationship might be a good idea.

Most people are lonely. And scared. The two go together. We know we need other people in our lives, but we're not sure anyone is there.

And yet our lives are filled with people. We bump into hundreds every day, in restaurants, in malls, in grocery stores, and in our places of business. We carry on conversations all the time: brief exchanges with checkout clerks, pleasant chats with acquaintances, intense dialogues with family and friends over plans or conflict. We're with people, and talking with them, a lot.

But still we're lonely. And scared. No one seems to really be there, not in the way we want. In honest moments, we relate to Stephen Crane's despair when he announced to the universe, "Sir, I exist!" only to hear the reply, "That, to me, is a matter of supreme indifference."

We want someone to answer differently, to hear our cry and come running, to listen to everything we're saying, not just to those parts that are easily handled. We want someone to demonstrate wise interest in our struggles, to cry when we make known our pain, to celebrate with our laughter, to stay strongly involved for the long haul.

But we're terrified of what we most want: to be known with neither secrets nor pretense. We would be willing to present our lives to someone if we were confident that that person cared and knew what to do. We want someone to be there when we hurt.

That someone used to be the "elder in the community," perhaps the pastor of a local congregation or the father in a family or wise older folks in a natural community. In some parts of Africa, that someone still is the elder. An African student in an American seminary was surprised to learn how often people in the West quickly turn to a psychologist for help. "In my church, I stood up at the end of the service and admitted to a personal struggle I could no longer handle. As soon as the service was over, several elders gathered around me, and we arranged

> But we're terrified of what we most want: to be known with neither secrets nor pretense.

extensive time to counsel together. Isn't that what the body of Christ should do?"

A psychologist in private practice in North America regularly asks Christians who come to him why they didn't go first to their pastor or elders for help. He reports that three of the most frequently given answers are:

1. "He does not relate very well."
2. "He seems to have a superficial approach to life."
3. "I have never talked to him about anything in depth, but I think he would tend to simplify my difficulties."

In modern western culture, when something goes wrong with our lives, we call a professional, sometimes right away, sometimes after other efforts to solve our problems have failed. When the difficulty reaches a certain level, we want nothing less than professional help. Chicken soup is good for a cold, but a physician's expertise is needed for pneumonia. Our pastor's counsel might get us over a glitch in our marriage, but big problems require specialized help. That's how we think.

To find the help we need, we turn to

people who meet at least three criteria:

1. They are willing to make available the necessary time for dealing meaningfully with our problems.
2. They must care enough to genuinely want to see us helped.
3. They must have both the necessary knowledge to accurately recognize what is wrong and the necessary skill to do whatever needs to be done.

In our culture, the person we perceive to best meet all three requirements is the professional therapist.

In the first chapters, I've explored the range of answers we give to the two questions we instinctively ask when problems arise in our lives: What's wrong? and Who can help? In this chapter I want to consider one more set of answers—the one that turns us toward therapy. Let's briefly review what we've said so far. It's important to keep the other options in mind because the decision to consult a therapist is often made after every other alternative to finding help has been tried and found wanting. The simple chart that follows—listing all the options—will help.

## If We Think Our Problems Are Caused by:

| | |
|---|---|
| OPTION #1:<br>**Personal<br>Sin** | Wrong choices; violation of moral standards; idolatry ⸱ the heart. |
| OPTION #2:<br>**Undisciplined<br>Living** | Sloppy habits; careless indulgence; inattention to everyday responsibilities and Christian duties. |
| OPTION #3:<br>**Spiritual<br>Warfare** | Satanic strongholds; demonic oppression; naiveté about the power of evil. |
| OPTION #4:<br>**Deficient<br>Spirituality** | Lukewarmness; lack of a diligent search for God; superficial attitude toward spiritual things. |
| OPTION #5:<br>**Biochemical<br>Disorder** | Chemical imbalance; genetic weakness; injury to brain; nerve damage. |
| OPTION #6:<br>**Psychological<br>Disorder** | Dysfunctional background; emotional trauma; buried memories; damaged sense of self. |

# Then We Will Turn for Help to:

| | |
|---|---|
| **Ourselves and God** | With God's help, we are responsible to confess, repent, and obey. Pastors, friends, and counselors may support and exhort us, but the decision is ours to live as we should. |
| **Ourselves** | We must prioritize, organize, and discipline our lives according to a plan that's good for our physical and spiritual lives. |
| **God** | Only God is stronger than the devil. Our job is to harness his resources to win the battle against evil principalities and powers. |
| **God** | We need to connect with God, to draw on every available means of grace. |
| **Medical Professionals** | Psychiatrists, neurologists, and other "body doctors" who specialize in treating emotional symptoms with an organic cause. |
| **Professional Counselor** | Psychotherapists, counselors, and social workers trained to uncover the roots of psychological distress and treat them. |

Let's look more closely at the sixth option. (To some degree, it overlaps with a few of the others.) If the cause of our problems is a psychological disorder brought on by a dysfunctional background, then the helper of choice is a professional therapist. More broadly, if the cause of our problems involves a nonmedical difficulty within our personal makeup, a disorder that is not easily or naturally understood, then the helper of choice is someone specially trained to deal with such problems. We often call that person a counselor or therapist.

The idea of "therapist" is relatively recent in our world. For centuries, spiritual leaders, wise elders, ordained

> **When the difficulty reaches a certain level, we want nothing less than professional help. Chicken soup is good for a cold, but a physician's expertise is needed for pneumonia.**

priests, and discerning friends have been called on for help when life became troublesome. Dependence on these sorts of helpers arose naturally from the way people understood their problems. Difficulties in living, if they did not originate in a medical condition, grew out of philosophical or religious shortcomings. People assumed that sufficient help was available in a communal context where both friends and leaders shared responsibility for the cure of souls.

Over time, our thinking shifted. We came to regard personal problems as symptoms of a complicated malfunction of internal forces. When that shift occurred, the community yielded its curative role to specialists who emerged from the community but who developed their expertise away from it. These specially trained helpers became the experts to whom people turned with problems that untrained folks in the community could not handle.

These experts banded together and formed a new community, professional associations that gradually replaced their original communities as primary sources of identity, values, and purpose. Many therapists, of course, are deeply committed Christians and faithful church members who rightly consider their work as service for Christ. But what they do is typically more rooted in their professional worlds than in their Christian communities. They may consult with church leadership and teach Sunday school class, but they remain professional therapists in private practice. Their identity, values, and purpose reflect their role as therapists more than as members of a local church.

The justifying assumption behind their work is that problems, though perhaps developed in community, are now located within the individual and can best be dealt with by a therapeutic relationship with one person. That assumption extends to say that the therapist is trained to do what cannot be done by anyone who is not a therapist. Like a dentist, a therapist may exhort certain behaviors to promote one's health during everyday life, but, it is assumed, certain problems are best handled during the professional appointment.

Tied to this way of thinking is the idea that it is the person who needs therapy, not the person-in-community who needs richer connection with his or her community. Psychological and spiritual needs have become the focus. No longer do we speak of needing something. Now we think of ourselves as having needs. The priority is seeing to it that personal needs are met.[1] When we hurt, we often assume that behind the pain are unmet needs. We define these unmet needs as the core of the psychological damage that must be repaired. Just as a broken leg must be healed before the runner can return to the race, so something inside the individual must be dealt with first in order to restore that individual to effective functioning in a group. And that is the job of therapy.

But what exactly does a therapist do? What is therapy? Do folks use the term wrongly when they say "Going fishing for a few days was the therapy I needed" or "Taking care of an elderly aunt was so therapeutic during the months after my husband left me"? Is

No longer do we speak of needing something. Now we think of ourselves as having needs. The priority is seeing to it that personal needs are met.

"therapeutic" the same as "helpful"? If so, is there a certain kind of conversation that is more therapeutic than others? And is that kind of conversation what therapists uniquely offer? What kind of training is required to learn to converse therapeutically? Or maybe it's less a matter of training and more a matter of character, something that is gained not in a classroom but through suffering.

Once we conclude that we need to see a therapist, the question naturally arises: What will the therapist do?

We know what to expect when we walk into a dentist's office. We've nervously crawled into several dentists' chairs. They're all pretty much the same—cushioned head rest, tilt mechanism controlled by a foot pedal, a round light dangling menacingly over our heads. Then the same words—"Open, please," followed by "A little wider. There! That's good. Now hold it open just like that for about an hour." Sharp instruments, a jiggled cheek while the needle pierces our gum, that infernal whirring of the drill, ice water squirted with laser precision on the exposed nerve.

When we go to a dentist, we know what to expect. The procedure is roughly the same because it is based on a body of scientific knowledge that every modern dentist has studied. And that's our confidence, that one dentist will proceed similarly to another because both studied the same textbook.

But things are not so predictable when we go to a therapist's office. Beyond comfortable chairs and the exchange of words, what happens varies widely among different therapists.

The general public isn't always aware that therapists differ as much as they do. Certainly good therapists share much in common. They listen well, they care, they understand the pain and struggle you're experiencing, and they want to help. And Christian therapists, of course, share basic doctrinal positions that define them as Christian.

But those commonalities provide broad boundaries within which there is plenty of room for widely differing theories about the nature of personal struggles and practices about dealing with them. When people turn to professional Christian therapists for help, they should realize that there is no real consensus about how therapy should be conducted. Professionals operate from a variety of viewpoints about what is wrong and what needs to be done.

Picking a therapist is like picking a restaurant. They all serve food, but the menus can be very different. In Part 3, Dr. Allender explores the major positions held by Christian therapists that determine what they do when someone comes to them for help.

# PART
# 3

# What Will
# the Helper Do?

# 9

# All Therapies Are Not Created Equal

c∞ɔ

W̱E LIVE IN AN increasingly chaotic, fragmented world. Personal and relational problems, at least, appear to be worse. We feel isolated from community, uncertain about what to do, and desperate for someone to lead us. For most, time is one of our most precious commodities, and few people have the time or context to listen for hours upon hours to our struggles.

Consequently, therapy appears to be "paid friendship" or "expert wisdom" that makes up for the busyness and superficiality of most relationships. To a degree, people seek counseling for explanations and solutions to their problems and for a connection that is not found in their routine relationships. Counseling offers not only connection and direction, but it offers what is so seldom experienced in daily life: caring, thoughtful, guided reflection on the soul's passion, direction, and struggle with God and others.

Counseling is an arena where people can grapple with their soul, relationships, and God. People seek counseling because they believe there are inner struggles that they cannot handle on their own. When they have tried to get help, people have minimized their symptoms. But inside, they still strug-

> **Counseling offers not only connection and direction, but it offers what is so seldom experienced in daily life: caring thoughtful, guided reflection on the soul's passion, direction, and struggle with God and others.**

gle, and this inner war is leading to personal and relational harm that does not change by "normal" channels of help (prayer, books, coffee conversations) or by "normal" consequences (pain, confrontation from others, loss of hope). Hurting people desperately want to be heard, understood, and invited to know God in the midst of their confusion. And so they turn to therapists for wisdom.

Is that what most clients gain when they see a therapist? In large part the answer to that question depends on the core assumptions that shape the therapist's perspective.

## CORE ASSUMPTIONS

It was once thought that counseling is a value-free relationship. For many years, therapists were trained to keep their values out of their work and allow the clients to form their own values and beliefs. But it became increasingly apparent that each psychotherapeutic system held divergent "beliefs" about the nature of humanity, problems, and change. Each approach to counseling therefore is a separate "religion" that seeks to convert the client to a different view of life consistent with its core assumptions.

A practitioner of a therapy that seeks to change negative thinking would ask different questions, emphasize different components of the human condition, and offer different techniques for change than a person who was trained to uncover the influences of unconscious conflict from one's past. Each therapist consciously or unwittingly holds to beliefs and values that shape their work with a client.

A person can't choose a therapist merely on the basis of location, cost, or professional license. It is imperative to know something about the therapist's core assumptions. Do they intend to be biblical? Do they intend to address the core issues of the soul as articulated in the Bible? Many Christian therapists see no need to integrate their professional practice with their religious convictions. They are followers of a psychological system, and their explanations of problems and solutions may overlap with some of the principles from the Bible, but their separation of practice and faith is problematic for those who want to heal the soul in light of the truth of the Bible.

> It is crucial to accept the limits of all help.

110

What are the core assumptions of those who offer professional help? My plan is not to offer a thorough analysis or critique of each approach, but to reflect on the central issues that drive professional therapy. Using stories, I reveal the assumptions that are found in dynamic therapy (chapter 10), recovery groups (chapter 11), and spiritual interventions (chapter 12). Finally, I explore how the professional counselor can uniquely aid the healing of the soul (chapter 14).

Janice, a woman I counseled, will serve as an illustration of the benefits and limits of each approach. Many times I will counsel people who have been in therapy before or who have sought other means to deal with their pressing concerns. At times people come to me because they are dissatisfied with the approach being offered by another therapist, but more often they sense that each person and approach has a season, a time of helpfulness, but more is needed. It is crucial to accept the limits of all help. Some of the limits are due to issues that are not acknowledged or integrated into the theory and practice of a particular model. More often than not, the limit is due to the tension that we were made for heaven and all help is time bound and incomplete. Nevertheless, it is imperative to ask the simple question: How can we be more biblical in our approach to understanding people, problems, and the process of change? To answer the question, we will follow some of Janice's story of seeking help.

## THE STORY OF JANICE

Janice confidently walked into my office. She picked a chair and said: "I suppose if this is your chair, you'll tell me." She glanced at the worn and faded arms of the chair I normally sat in, looked back at the pinkish couch I had picked up thirteen years ago at a going-out-of business sale, stared back at me, and said: "I hope you're a better therapist than interior designer." There was no humor to her voice. It was firm, direct, and tinged with barely hidden sarcasm. I liked her.

I asked how I could be of help. She had recently ended another destructive relationship; her boyfriend had physically abused her and used her in countless ways. She had gone to talk to her pastor, and his counsel had been to break off the relationship, change her phone number, and get into a small group study led by one of the older women in the church.

This group had nurtured Janice and

prayed with her when she felt the irresistible pull to return to her boyfriend. Like countless other men she had dated, he seemed to have the power to shift her tides and draw her back into the same destructive patterns that the day before she had recognized as near suicidal.

Janice was a top executive with a powerful lobbying firm. She traveled all over the country and spoke before legislatures, political parties, and in closed-door negotiation sessions. She was used to being in control; she lived in the fast lane. But she was also a believer and sickened by her controlled, chaotic, empty, busy life. She wanted help.

When I asked how I could be of help, she said, "Who knows? Do you? What do you have to offer for ninety dollars an hour that I can't get from a good book, my Bible study, my pastor, or my crazy aunt who believes I am God's gift to the universe? I have been in therapy several times; I have had demons cast out of me by some well-meaning friends, done the recovery thing, and now been in a Bible study group. So how will this be different?"

Janice may have asked the question more pointedly than most, but she voiced what the vast majority of people ask when they consider therapy. Why? What am I going to get? What is so different about this "hour" that will help?

My answer was "little." The brevity of my answer and my ease with her directness put her at ease and she said: "Fine." Then she told me the last few months had brought her to feel that her Bible study, aunt, pastor, books, and friends were not addressing her urge to return to her destructive past boyfriend.

She slumped in my chair and sighed deeply. "I know they love me and mean well," she said, "but they see so many of my good qualities that no one really seems to believe that I am that dark or disturbed. No one wants to take me seriously. And when they do, they seem to panic and offer quick advice or truths that just don't seem to reach deep enough or long enough to change something I can't put my finger on."

In her quest for healing, Janice had already sought the help of therapists, recovery groups, and spiritual intervention. While she found a measure of healing in each one, ultimately each approach seemed to fall short of truly addressing her problems.

Janice provides a clear window into the

benefits and liabilities of the three approaches typically used by the Christian therapeutic community: dynamic therapy, recovery or twelve-step groups, and spiritual intervention. As I share Janice's experience with these three methods, I do not intend to outline and critique each approach. Instead, I hope to show how each model addresses issues that are crucial to understand if our soul is to find healing.

# 10

# Dynamic Therapy: Recovering and Healing Our Past

⸎

BEFORE SHE BEGAN THERAPY, Janice had memories of a number of incidents of past sexual abuse, but she had never considered those events as being related to her current struggles. She was equally aware that her family had been a hostile and lonely place to grow up. Her mother was a cold, efficient, busy woman, and her father was a generous but weak man who would never stand up for his daughter in family fights, nor express his concern about her mother's periodic rages.

When Janice began therapy, she was

116

convinced her family was both normal and average, her childhood reasonably happy. It is not uncommon for people who have suffered significant abuse and neglect to consider their past as unexceptional and unrelated to their current struggles. Her therapist, who approached therapy from a dynamic perspective, helped her name her experiences in her family and invited her to feel hurt, anger, and loss. He further helped her interpret the past abuse as damaging to her self-esteem; he invited her to mourn over the loss of her innocence and feel anger over the absence of protecting parents.

This therapist employed the dynamic approach to counseling. Dynamic therapy typically looks at three key issues: (1) unconscious motivation, (2) repressed traumatic/fantasized memories, and (3) the importance of the transference relationship for healing. After discussing each issue I will evaluate them from a biblical perspective.

## UNCONSCIOUS MOTIVATION

Dynamic theories assume that our choices, our direction in life, and our personality are mostly an involuntary, unconscious response to internal conflict. According to classic Freudian dynamic theory, the young boy is attracted to his mother, but he represses that sexual attraction in his unconscious because he is afraid that his father will castrate him.

The young girl is attracted to her father, but represses that attraction for fear of conflict with her mother. Most dynamic therapists today would see the basic drive not as sexual, but relational, and the basic anxiety as not fear of castration, but fear of absorption or abandonment. But while they disagree on the details, most dynamic therapists hold to the theory that people repress conflict into the unconscious.

The unconscious is viewed as a storage center of unbidden desires, fantasies, and memories that put one in danger with an important caregiver, family, or community. This center controls a person's

> *Insight releases repression and allows for catharsis—the feeling and expression of a wide range of backlogged emotions.*

choices. Her unconscious molds how she perceives and assesses data without her even knowing. For example, due to past repressed trauma, a woman may interpret all relational tenderness as dangerous and all potential harm as safe. Her unconscious is like defective computer software that reads all numbers in reverse order. Her "wiring" is crossed, and she is unaware of this malfunction that distorts her experience.

The task of the dynamic therapist is to release the repression and allow access to the unconscious, thus freeing up choice and increasing creativity. Most dynamic therapists do this by observing how the client responds in the therapeutic hour and by offering interpretive insights about the past. Insight releases repression and allows for catharsis—the feeling and expression of a wide range of backlogged emotions. Insight and emotional expression unclog the psychic pipes and bring more humanity to the rigid soul.

Janice's therapist often made connections between the past and present. She told me about one of their interactions:

> Janice: I don't know why you can't tell me your opinion as to what I should do about my

boyfriend's constant demands to have sex with him.

Dr. Smithson: What are you feeling, Janice?

Janice: I'm irritated with you. I don't know what is right and what is wrong anymore, and I don't feel like you will help me.

Dr. Smithson: Janice, close your eyes and use your frustration to help you remember how you felt when your father sat by idly as your mother yelled at you.

Dr. Smithson was using guided imagery to attempt to release the hurt and confusion Janice felt as a young girl. He assumed that her frustration with him in the moment had deeper roots to the past and that an answer to the current struggle might block her from facing the real issue involved in her confusion: the unacknowledged desire for a father who would take care of her.

Dr. Smithson assumes our distorted past keeps us from knowing the truth. The Bible places the reason we do not face truth on a different ground. I do not want to face the truth about myself, others, or life because truth is not only painful, but humbling. Facing our past involves struggling with our

120

sorrow and confusion over the harm that God did not prevent and seeing our ugly attempts to make life work without God. We know truth—the heavens declare the glory of God and the internal witness of our conscience convicts—but we choose to ignore truth and become ignorant, blind, and hard.

Is there an unconscious? Yes, but it is only incidentally the repository of unbidden, dangerous, or merely frightening fantasies or memories; it is far more the storehouse of independent, self-willed energy to be a god and to control our world no matter what the consequence. Its core function is to hide our flight and fight against God. In that sense, the unconscious is our capacity to deceive others and ourselves in order to ignore or distort our relationship with God.

The biblical "dynamist" will reveal our

I do not want to face the truth about myself, others, or life because truth is not only painful, but humbling.

unconscious flight from truth by showing how our current relational patterns are connected to our history. They will look at our current effort to create a god of our own making. Once we have faced our own lies, the door opens to clearer choices. Dr. Smithson could have moved in this direction:

> Janice: I don't know why you can't tell me your opinion as to what I should do about my boyfriend's constant demands to have sex with him.
>
> Dr. Smithson: Janice, I can easily answer that question. I suspect you are quite clear about what the Bible teaches about premarital sexual involvement.
>
> Janice: Yes, but I feel so confused. Can't you at least tell me how to get out of this mess?
>
> Dr. Smithson: You are frustrated with me. When you feel confused, your pattern has been to demand that someone older and wiser give you what your dad never would offer. If someone does, you find some way to thwart it. If someone doesn't, you

seem to feel justified to do as you want. And that is usually to put yourself in harm's way. Then you can blame yourself and God. Janice, do you want to deal with this issue rather than merely sit in your confusion and frustration?

If Dr. Smithson had moved in this direction in his therapy, he would have invited Janice to look at horizontal patterns of relating to others in light of what her heart demands from God. Janice wants answers. She wants strong, clear direction, and when it is not forthcoming, it seems like she gives up the hope of making good decisions on her own. In turn, the hopelessness gives way to an invitation to others to use her, and then she reenters the vicious cycle of personal sabotage.

It is never enough to merely pursue God—we must do so in light of our efforts to make life work apart from trusting him. But it is equally an error to face horizontal life patterns without seeing the vertical dimension—that is, our demands of God. At times, we refuse to face reality in either dimension. The dynamic model appropriately assumes there is much about reality that we do not want to face. One path to facing reality involves facing the context of how we formed our earliest views of life and relationship.

## REPRESSED TRAUMATIC/ FANTASIZED MEMORIES

The dynamic model assumes that the structure of our personality is formed in the early years of our life by the kind of parenting we received. The memories of love or neglect construct the core of our self-assessment and self-esteem. If our memories are tainted with violence, sexual abuse, abandonment, absorption, or verbal abuse, then they are repressed in the unconscious. But they continue to influence us by being our only map for journeying through life.

Repression is the mechanism that deposits the scenes of the past into the reservoir of the unconscious. Repression of painful memories can be compared to a rock being thrown into quicksand. The rock's weight will naturally, without effort, cause it to sink to the bottom. In the same way, painful data is too difficult to remember, and therefore it is forgotten.

The core material "forgotten" involves fantasized[1] or actual scenes of violence or sex. These memories are repressed, causing the conscience (superego) to become rigid

124

and dictatorial. If we can accept the normalcy of our fantasies and memories, then the repression is lifted, and the past can be reintegrated into the present.

The task of the dynamic therapist is to draw the past to the surface through techniques of free association, age regression, dream analysis, or hypnosis. The task is to make what is unconscious conscious and then embrace what is known as normal.

Janice: I felt so angry at my mother. She was a witch. And Daddy was so busy, he just didn't know what was going on. He would have helped me if he had known what I was going through.

The task of the dynamic therapist is to draw the past to the surface through techniques of free association, age regression, dream analysis, or hypnosis.

125

Dr. Smithson: Janice, see if you can recall one time when your mother was yelling at you.

Janice: Well, one comes to mind. It was right after my twelfth birthday party. Someone gave me a bra as a joke and my mother was scandalized, but she would never say anything while the other kids were there. When they left, she tore me up one side and down the other for having dirty-minded friends like that.

Dr. Smithson: Where was your father? Was he at the party?

Janice: I suppose. I don't remember.

Dr. Smithson: You suppose, but don't remember. Do you suppose he saw all that occurred?

Janice: Yeah, maybe.

Dr. Smithson: It would be too painful for you to face that your father not only saw the embarrassing moment of receiving the bra, but also saw and heard your mother's rage. And he did nothing.

Dr. Smithson seems to assume that the

real problem lies in a forgotten memory of emotional abuse. Due to the great pain of the past, Janice is unable to face her memories and therefore is doomed to repeat them in abusive relationships.

The Bible does suggest that we suppress the truth in unrighteousness (Romans 1:18–21). Suppression is, in simple terms, hiding. We take truth and push it under the water so we can no longer see it in its simple, direct witness. We consciously refuse to be humbled by the weight of God's glory. One ought to look at a sunrise and be aware that an infinite and merciful being has painted our existence with order, wonder, and beauty. Then we ought to realize that we are his handiwork, created for his glory. Such an awareness ought to simultaneously humble us and enlarge our sense of gratitude.

But when we refuse to see and refuse to be humbled and grateful, then we escape the call to give glory to God. As such, suppression is a forgetting of truth.

We forget two central things: (1) events that cause us to question the goodness of God, and (2) our response of rebellion that is an attempt to control a chaotic life and an unmanageable God. Dynamic theories presume we repress due to pain; the Bible states we suppress due to idolatry. Dynamic theories assume we repress sexuality and violence. So does the Bible. Jesus said the two greatest struggles of the soul are lust (adultery) and anger (murder) (Matthew 5:21–28). In both adultery and murder we abdicate true worship and pursue the idols of our own making.

Idolatry is not the by-product of forgetting God; it is the means by which we forget him. I don't merely misplace God. Instead, I forget God by turning my heart to gods that seem to provide for my soul far better than God. When I center myself on those gods, then the true God fades into the background and then out of my consciousness.

The biblical "dynamist's" task is to expose the heart's inclination to suppress truth and link the content of our memory or fantasy to our adulterous and violent desire to be a god. Dr. Smithson could have done that in his conversation with Janice by exposing her flight from the truth.

Dr. Smithson: It would be too painful for you to face that your father not only saw the embarrassing moment of receiving the bra, but that he saw and heard your mother's rage. And he did nothing.

Janice: Yes, maybe, but he didn't like conflict, and I can't blame him. I didn't like interacting with my mother either.

Dr. Smithson: Of course, but you did fight. You chose to fight, but then you turned against yourself to keep yourself from facing your hurt with your mom and the bitter sense of betrayal you felt when your father refused to protect you. Janice, this is only a part of the picture. You just fought me to get me off the track of your father's betrayal. And I can't help but think you do the same mental gymnastics with God.

Here Dr. Smithson is assuming that Janice's way of relating to her father also revealed something about the heart of her relationship with God. True biblical therapy will draw forth the nature of our relationships with others in part to explore the nature of our desires, illusions, and demands that have to do with God.

# IMPORTANCE OF THE TRANS-FERENCE RELATIONSHIP FOR HEALING

The dynamic model assumes we will live out the same repetitive patterns in relationships until the repression is lifted and the unconscious is freed. We will live out those patterns most intensely in relationships that elicit memories of past conflict involving shame, loss, and betrayal. Those memories of harm become the basis of how we see ourselves and others. A child who was repeatedly mocked for being overweight will seldom have an accurate and accepting body image. This is especially true if a parent was the prime source of the trauma. The parent's face, words, and actions will color the way the child judges herself and structures her sense of value, morality, and beauty.

For this reason, the dynamic model argues that the past will resurface in a relationship that parallels the original trauma. This is called in therapy the "transference neurosis." Past harm will show in the current relationship with the therapist if the therapist is a relatively blank screen on which the client can project her inner conflicts.

The transference from the past to the present is like a movie of the past being "projected" onto the blank screen of the therapist. If there are too many marks on the screen, then the past projections will be contaminated and the transference of the past to the present relationship with the therapist will not occur. The dynamic therapist provides a neutral, professional relationship to the client as he interprets this data. As a result the client's anxiety decreases as she "takes in" the therapist as a safe, caring alternative to the hostile, abandoning parent. After many, many repeated experiences, the soul begins to restructure itself by replacing the destructive images of the past with current images of respect and care. After many years, healing takes place.

The Bible assumes as well that we change in the context of relationships. Further, the Bible assumes that what is in our heart will be revealed in the way we conduct ourselves in relationship with others. Do we distort current relationships due to past pain? Of course, but the issue is not merely horizontal; it is vertical. The real distortion of relationship arises in our effort to avoid seeing what is true about our heart toward God.

The apostle John links what is true about our human relationships to our relationship with God.

We know that we have passed from death to life, because we love our brothers. Anyone who does not love remains in death. Anyone who hates his brother is a murderer, and you know that no murderer has eternal life in him. This is how we know what love is: Jesus Christ laid down his life for us. And we ought to lay down our lives for our brothers. (1 John 3:14–16)

Our worst human relationship will determine the quality of our relationship with God, says John. In human relationships we see most clearly our deepest struggles with God. It is not possible to say, "I trust God," and then trust no other human being; or "I love God," and love no other human being. What is true about our heart direction with human beings will reveal what our heart believes about God.

Further, the Bible assumes that change in our relationship with God will occur in direct proportion to our change in relationships with others. Relationship with God grows when we move to bless others with the gift of life that we have first received from God. To the degree we love others, the more we will know about the heart of God (John 15:10–14).

The process of change is by necessity relational. The core to change is not "taking in" the therapist as a good parent, but rather releasing our redeemed instinct to love.

The task of the biblical "dynamist" is to enter deeply into relationship with the client in order to draw forth and expose the confusion, ambivalence, and hatred that blocks relationship with God.

The therapist invites the client to see the unique history that has shaped her demand to find life apart from trusting God and loving others. The biblical "dynamist" stands as a link between the past and the future revealing the role of trauma in shaping our view of God and others. But it is never enough to merely see how we have been damaged by trauma; we must also face what we have done to make our own gods given that God did not seem to come through for us. The biblical dynamist exposes our

**Our worst human relationship will determine the quality of our relationship with God.**

heart's flight from God and our demand that we be a god.

## EVALUATION OF THE DYNAMIC MODEL

Janice changed during her therapy. She was able to break off a destructive relationship with an abusive man. She had more energy for her work, and she began to take care of herself through a change in her diet, sleep habits, and friendships. Her self-esteem rose, and she began to enjoy life. After two years of therapy, she terminated therapy when most of her symptoms were either resolved or significantly reduced.

The therapist helped Janice see that she was extremely hostile to other women and refused to develop friendships for fear of competition and conflict. She clearly saw that her view of women was strongly shaped by her aggressive, critical, punishing mother. She also discovered that she tended to take care of seductive, needy men. She was still defensive about seeing this pattern as an outworking of her relationship with her father, but she did relate her "codependency" to her role of being his caretaker.

She also learned that, due to the past sexual abuse, she equated sex with love.

Through therapy, she learned that she was not responsible for the abuse that occurred, but her therapist did not spend much time talking about the ripple effects of the past sexual abuse on her current relationships. Nevertheless, the therapist had helped her see that it was legitimate to feel sexual arousal without acting on the impulse. Further, she also learned to interpret sexual arousal as a signal for wanting to be held or enjoyed.

According to her, Janice neither grew nor turned away from God during her therapy. God was mostly irrelevant to the process. The task of healing her psyche had no effect on the direction of her soul.

Janice never really saw her struggle with men, her parents, or her past sexual abuse as idolatrous worship, suppression of the truth

> The past is not something to forget or ignore, because our views of ourselves, others, and God are formed from the wounds of the past.

in unrighteousness, nor flight from God. Her therapist made a fairly strong division between psychological problems and spiritual issues. If one struggles with prayer, or with trusting God, then one has a spiritual problem. But if the struggles involve relational problems or symptoms of internal conflict, then one has a psychological problem. This division leads to a radically different course of treatment. Most dynamic therapists hold to this division.

Was Janet helped by her dynamic therapist? Absolutely. She saw her past in a new light, and her heart was open to looking at her life with more honesty and integrity. She began to make healthy decisions in relationships, and she learned to grieve and take better care of herself.

Dynamic therapy can take a person a long way on the road to healing because it acknowledges that the past is deeply grooved into our present. The past is not something to forget or ignore, because our views of ourselves, others, and God are formed from the wounds of the past. But dynamic therapy usually stops before inviting the client to face what she has done with God. Symptoms, like eating disorders, are simply seen as dysfunctional ways of finding relief and happiness.

This view does not look deeply enough into the dark, shadow sides of human dysfunction. As often practiced, the dynamic model highlights human dignity rather than delving into the depths of idolatry and human depravity. Consequently, God is either ignored, or merely seen as one of the prime agents for encouraging the healing process. He becomes the therapist's ally to support and cheer on the psychological healing process conducted by the therapist.

As a consequence, there were many issues Janice was not compelled to face. She somehow avoided grappling with her hatred of hope and glory. She was terrified of feeling innocent, lovely, and strong. Her ambivalent relationship with her father and her experience of sexual abuse with a neighbor had led her to unconsciously presume there would never be a moment of rest and joy with a man. She was either the savior or the victim; she played both roles well.

In part, she did not deal with those elements due to her therapist's refusal to expose how deeply she hated the hunger God had put in her as a woman. She hated her passions; therefore she warred against God by fighting against herself.

Sadly, less than a year after her therapy,

she was back in an abusive relationship with a seductive man. This relationship continued on and off for several years. After much duress, she sought spiritual help from her pastor and was invited to join a women's Bible study. It was one of her first opportunities to study the Bible, enjoy fellowship with women, and feel accountable to other human beings. She felt greater courage to break off the relationship, but often slipped back into the destructive patterns when the urge to reconnect to him occurred.

## TRUE SOUL CARE

The soul will not be healed without truth. The soul hungers for truth and naturally hates lies—we hate false advertising, dishonest friends, or societal pretense. We hate falsehood until we are caught in our own lies. We see dishonesty and long for truth until the truth requires us to be humbled and stripped of our hiding place. True soul care offers truth in the gentle, probing light of grace. Truthing in love is not a violent blow of vitriol that crushes the heart, but a piercing cut to the core that reveals our need for forgiveness.

Healing the soul requires the disruption of our most deeply imbedded lies and illusions. Healing does not occur as long as we are free to manipulate life to gain what only God can provide; he offers what we long for only in the context of brokenness. God can only be approached and known in desperate need, without demand or condition. When our most intimate and subtle efforts to make ourselves god are exposed and disrupted, we finally are broken.

> The soul will not be healed without truth.

No wonder Proverbs says "Faithful are the wounds of a friend," for the soul healer is a friend who befriends us not to win us, use us, or merely to enjoy us, but to see us become like the God we are to imitate (Ephesians 5:1ff.). Therefore, we must understand the labyrinth-like, blind-alley routes of idolatry. We must be sin experts. The training ground comes from our personal wrestling with idolatry and suppression of the truth. It is further amplified by relating the core of idolatry to manifold symptoms of personal struggle, such as eating disorders, sexual problems, gossip, poor self-esteem, ad infinitum.

Who will be this kind of disrupter? It will be a person who has seen rich hope rise in the midst of personal despair. It will be one who has seen God cut through the complexity of depravity to reveal the righteous simplicity of repentance. The soul healer will be one who is willing to use the Bible and life experience to reveal the heart.

> The soul healer is a friend who befriends us not to win us, use us, or merely to enjoy us, but to see us become like the God we are to imitate.

But exposure alone is deadly. A person who sees himself as a prophetic/disruptive force in another person's life must also be a person who glories in grace, tenderness, and long-suffering. If his life is not equally disrupted and open to exposure, then he will be enamored by his cleverness and arrogantly indulge in pontificating on the complexities of the human soul. The prophetic/disruptive biblical "dynamist" must also be more enamored by the simple wonder of forgiveness than the need for change.

For that reason, the recovery model brings to light another element that is crucial if the heart is to know hope. Every person longs to experience the embrace of acceptance and a greater taste of the wonder of forgiveness. Recovery groups often provide people their first moments of shame-free rest and the restoration of hope. The next chapter will explore the benefits of the recovery movement.

# 11

# Recovery Movement: Letting Our Shame Go

❦

SOON AFTER JANICE QUIT therapy a good friend invited her to a recovery group that met in the basement of her church. At first, Janice deferred. She said: "I am not an addict. No one in my family is addicted to alcohol or sex." But her friend handed her a sheet of paper that detailed the characteristics of someone who is addicted. She fit ten out of twelve characteristics. She was hooked and a week later attended her first meeting.

The group was warm and honest. They asked her to introduce herself and she was applauded for coming. Nothing was asked

142

of her, and she felt no pressure to talk. A few people introduced themselves with their first names and then usually a word or phrase that stated their addiction. "Hi, I'm Jim, and I am an addict." "Hi, I'm Betsy, and I am also in recovery."

The introductions were lame but sincere, and Janice felt like she was watching a skit from "Saturday Night Live." But her suspicion and tough reserve melted slightly as person upon person rose to talk about their week, their recovery, and their struggles. There was a genuine sense of celebration she had never experienced during church or in any other place. She was really hooked.

Janice began a process that lasted almost two years. She went from hit-and-miss attendance to coming to the group two and sometimes three times a week. Eventually she was assigned a sponsor who had gone through the steps years before but continued to be in recovery and guide others through it as well. She also saw a female therapist who specialized in personalizing the recovery process through individual therapy.

In contrast to the dynamic therapy, she understood the language, had coaddicts who joined her and guided her in the journey, and knew what needed to be done over a lengthy apprenticeship as she did the steps. And best of all, the group work was free—in so many different ways.

Early in the process, Janice noticed that everyone was the same; everyone was addicted. There was no shame, no sense of judgment nor condemnation. She felt understood, cared for, and loved.

The contrast was so painful when she went to church on Sunday morning. The well-dressed men and women sang hymns and shook each other's hands with sincerity and warmth. When the pastor said to greet those sitting around you, Janice repeatedly shook hands and introduced herself to people she sat near most every Sunday. But no one remembered her name or face. No one ever asked her a question about her life. It felt more hollow than riding on a bus with a group of strangers she was not supposed to know. She continued to go to church, but her heart was in her recovery group.

Through the recovery group, individual therapy, and the literature of the movement, she learned for the first time about (1) shame and her dysfunctional family, (2) boundaries and taking care of herself, and (3) addiction and "doing the steps."

144

# SHAME AND DYSFUNCTIONAL FAMILIES

The real killer of the self and the real cause of all addictions is shame. Shame, according to this approach, is the experience of feeling deficient. Shame causes us to see our identity as flawed rather than seeing ourselves as having flaws. Our harsh judgments lead us to see ourselves as ugly, stupid, and fat. The result is a deep hole in the soul.

The shame-based person will often neglect himself and allow others to have control of his life. As pain increases, the victim of shame gravitates to objects, ideas, or persons that medicate the pain. Before long, shame propels the person into addiction.

Janice never had thought of herself as struggling with shame. In fact, when the topic came up she felt sad for those who felt so bad about themselves. She knew she strug-

> **Shame causes us to see our identity as flawed rather than seeing ourselves as having flaws.**

gled with going back into destructive relationships. She also fought an ongoing battle with masturbation, and she occasionally abused alcohol, but she never thought about what drove her to return to her destructive behavior. In fact, like most people, she never even thought of those struggles as addictions. She just figured she lacked self-control. She never connected her shame or her destructive patterns to her family.

There is little question that Janice's family was shame-based. Her mother was critical and punitive. Her father coddled her and was affirming unless her mother was present, then he was distant and silent. Janice knew that her father loved her but was afraid of provoking her mother's anger. In certain moments, Janice could admit her mother may have been jealous of her relationship with her father.

When the sexual abuse occurred, she felt more estranged from her family and sadly more distant from her father. It was during that time she began to masturbate more often. She felt dirty, but it was all that provided a sense of warmth and security. She never told anyone about the abuse and certainly she never admitted to anyone she struggled with sexual fantasies. But when it

146

came to the surface with her therapist, Martha, she felt enormous relief and freedom.

> Martha: Janice, you talk about the masturbation like you are disgusting and cheap.
>
> Janice: I, I just know I am wrong. I do feel cheap. My fantasies make me feel so dirty.
>
> Martha: It is not only normal to fantasize and express yourself sexually, but it is good.
>
> Janice: But then why do I feel so guilty?
>
> Martha: You feel guilty because you have let others define what is good for you. It is also due to the fact you have never forgiven yourself for the past sexual abuse. You were not responsible. It was not your fault, but you need to forgive your body for having felt arousal. Janice, what you are feeling is just what anybody would feel if they had such a critical, shaming family and if they had lost their inno-

cence and childhood through sexual abuse.

Shame is the toxic seed implanted by the failure of others. It will linger silently under the ground for years, but it will inevitably surface through a variety of addictions. In order to recover from shame, it is imperative to break the silence and confess one's addiction(s) and powerlessness to stop the cycle of shame and addiction. The structure provided by the Twelve Steps of Alcoholics Anonymous serves as a passageway to recover dignity, hope, and self-confidence.

The Bible talks a great deal about shame. The Old and New Testaments refer to the experience, context, and by-products of shame more than two hundred times. But the Bible does not view shame in the same way as many do in the recovery movement.

Shame does not arise merely from the mockery, the failure, or the dysfunction of others—it is an internal indication that we have put our faith in a god who is not God. Shame is the horror of being seen by another as a fool who has trusted in an idol that has failed us at our moment of need.

148

Isaiah summarizes the Bible's view of the relationship between idolatry and shame. "All who make idols are nothing," says Isaiah, "and the things they treasure are worthless. Those who would speak up for them are blind; they are ignorant, to their own shame. Who shapes a god and casts an idol, which can profit him nothing? He and his kind will be put to shame; craftsmen are nothing but men" (Isaiah 44:9–11).

An idol is anything we put our trust in to protect us and provide for our needs apart from God. It is the condition of heart that says: "This [object, idea, talent, or person] will give me life and keep me safe." Idolatry inevitably leads to fear and humiliation because it exposes us as

> Shame does not arise merely from the mockery, the failure, or the dysfunction of others—it is an internal indication that we have put our faith in a god who is not God.

equally blind, worthless, and ignorant.

Janice faced the presence and power of shame in her life. She acknowledged her mother was very critical, her father solicitous. She came to grips with how dirty she felt due to the past sexual abuse, but she had never thought about how she used her family and the past abuse to construct idols that enabled her to trust in herself rather than turning to God.

Often the view of shame taught in recovery circles leads to seeing ourselves as primarily a victim of past harm. Indeed many of us are victims, and victimization does do terrible damage to our hearts. But this view of shame does not take into account the core of shame: we are idolaters who pursue false gods irrespective of our past, our family, and our environment. Our past offers us the context in which we form unwitting, blind allegiance to idols to take away our loneliness and our heartache. These gods may work for a time, but they inevitably lead to even greater terror and infamy.

For example, Janice put her heart and trust in men's response to her. She knew she was perky and attractive. She loved to turn the eyes of men she did not know. Even more, she loved to spar verbally with a man who found her attractive. She liked to attract a man, then unnerve him with both her wit and her body.

But when a man became bored with her, she would do almost anything to keep him attracted. Her relationships with abusive men could be traced to this pattern. If a man was unkind, she would work harder to win him. When he turned to another woman, she would jealously pursue and provoke him. She had never faced this pattern of idolatry; no one in her recovery group wanted her to feel any more shame, and so her patterns of idolatry were never addressed. Therefore, her path to find life without God was never connected to her battle with God. Shame is not the cause of our struggles, but the sign of our deepest struggle: idolatrous movement away from God.

## BOUNDARIES AND TAKING CARE OF ONESELF

If our core problem is shame from our dysfunctional, shame-based family system, then the cure is to limit the harm and learn to take care of ourselves in nondestructive, self-enhancing ways. Boundary building is a major tenet of the recovery movement. Victims of shame are said to have porous or non-

> **Boundary setting is the capacity to say no when it is not my desire or in my best interest to do what you want; or to say yes to someone when it is both wise and mutually satisfying and healthy to do so.**

existent self boundaries; therefore others are free to walk through the unlocked door to steal, rape, and murder. On the other hand, a person with poor boundaries will "sacrifice" themselves for a pittance of involvement.

Boundary setting is the capacity to say no when it is not my desire or in my best interest to do what you want; or to say yes to someone when it is both wise and mutually satisfying and healthy to do so. A boundary is a limit that acknowledges respect for oneself and others. A person with poor boundaries may take a phone call from a friend when she is too tired to talk. Instead of respecting the limits of exhaustion, the person with poor boundaries will avoid hurting the friend and remain on the phone. The result will be greater exhaustion and erosion of self-respect.

In her therapy sessions, Martha helped Janice face her inclination to let others violate her boundaries.

> Janice: I was talking to my mom, and she just pounded me with guilt for not coming home for vacation.
>
> Martha: What did you say to her?
>
> Janice: Nothing. I just listened and finally she wore me down, and so I am going to go home for a while rather than heading East with my roommate.
>
> Martha: Janice, you let her control you. I bet after the phone call you did something harmful to yourself, like binge or stay up late.
>
> Janice: Wait a minute. How did you know that?
>
> Martha: It will happen almost every time you let your mother, or others, violate you with shame

and then determine your choice. Your boundaries are almost nonexistent, and so you let people rob you of dignity and self-respect. Janice, you are no different than most folks in recovery. We lack strong, clear boundaries. Do you want to go home?

Janice: No, not at all.

Martha: Then you need to call her back and set a clear boundary. First of all, she needs to know that you will not tolerate her shaming you and making you feel guilty. If she does it again, you need to tell her you will hang up. Second, you need to make a decision about what you really want to do and then stick with it.

Boundary building is an effort to circle the wagons to protect against harm long enough to bind up the wounds and restore health. It follows the oft-cited dictum: You have to learn to love yourself before you can love others. As one client said to me: "I have to learn to say no a lot, then I will come to distinguish what I want and what I don't want."

There is great truth in respecting boundaries, but building one's own boundaries misses a central biblical assessment: I don't lack in self-love; in fact, my self-love and my trust in my capacity to make and use idols has taken my past shame and victimization and made it much worse. The problem is never one of not setting boundaries. My problem is that I do not respect and love others.

The Bible asserts that love has its own natural boundaries; if we love, it is not to be at the expense of true respect for the other. For example, to assume a parent cannot bear the disappointment when we say we choose to do what they don't want is both presumptuous and disrespectful. And if our parent is hurt or angry then it is a matter for discussion, not time for an apology or submission to her demands. Love honors the other with a heart to do her good; it is not the avoidance of conflict, nor compliant servitude.

Love is not making someone feel good; it is not avoiding conflict; it is not merely getting along. Love is a commitment to see Christ grow in the heart of the other by offering a strength that disrupts patterns of idolatry and a tenderness that invites rec-

> **Love will be tender and long-suffering; it will also be bold and wounding. If it involves one without the other, then it is an offer of something less than God's character.**

onciliation and hope. Love will be tender and long-suffering; it will also be bold and wounding. If it involves one without the other, then it is an offer of something less than God's character. We are told that God is a God of mercy and strength (Psalm 62:11). To love others is to give them a taste of the full character of God.

Is it possible to love too much according to this notion? Of course not. Is something other than love necessary? Love may not be sufficient to soften a rebellious heart, but it is all that is needed to offer a taste of God. How then do we come to love more and more?

Jesus made the simplest connection between love and idolatry when he said: "He who has been forgiven little, loves little" (Luke 7:47). The other side of the coin holds equally true: He who is forgiven much, loves much. The assumption is not that we need to affirm ourselves so we can love others; instead, we need to be unnerved by the wonder of being forgiven. To know any portion of true love liberates the heart to want to return it in gratitude.

There is no greater joy than offering back the gift we have first received. The apostle John at the end of his life said: "I have no greater joy than to hear that my children are walking in the truth" (3 John 4). The soul is healed as it intentionally moves into the biblical drama of love. When we love, we walk into the mysterious, eternal purposes of God. The soul is healed as it is won in love and set free to touch others for purposes that reach to eternity.

## ADDICTION AND "DOING THE STEPS"

One of the most controversial elements of the recovery movement is its view about addiction. Three dominant assumptions provoke strong reaction: (1) everyone is addicted to something, (2) no one ever becomes totally unaddicted, and (3) freedom in (not from) addiction is a lifetime process of "doing the steps."

An addiction is an overwhelming urge to fill our emptiness with an object (e.g., food, alcohol), person (e.g., sex, codependency), or an ideology (perfectionism, religion). An addiction is a "disease." It is something that we can't help or control, and it is due to the "hole in the soul" related to our dysfunctional family or the by-product of our physiological makeup.

An addiction, according to this view, is not our fault—it is a given of existence. Our responsibility is getting into recovery. One axiom of the movement speaks to this responsibility: "If you are not in recovery, then you are part of the problem." An addict can't escape the struggle of addiction, but he can ameliorate the shame and fill the emptiness in a way that decreases the craving.

As long as an addict remains faithful to the process of recovery (the Twelve Steps) and to the people of recovery (the Twelve-Step group), then he can avoid the destructive depths of addiction. More often than not when one stops doing the steps and stops attending a recovery group, the insidious allure of addiction will creep back in, and over time the addictive cycle of craving-indulgence-shame-secrecy will seduce the addict back into the pit.

The central issue regarding this view of addiction is a matter of language. This may at first sound either too academic or too simplistic. If one reads recovery books and transposes these words—sin/idolatry for addiction; sanctification for recovery; repentance for powerlessness; Word of God instead of Twelve Steps; Jesus Christ instead of "higher power"; and church rather than recovery group—then recovery theory takes on a different focus.

Is the issue merely one of semantics? Is the recovery movement an attempt to evangelize in a language that most can understand rather than to speak in religious words that make little sense and unnecessarily offend before the person can comprehend what is being said?

The answer is complex. The original movement of Alcoholics Anonymous began as a result of alcoholics neither being welcome in the church, nor comprehending the Bible in light of their addictive compulsions. They were told they were drunks and simply needed to trust the Lord and choose to be different. In other words, they were shamed by self-righteous, blind Pharisees who neither faced their own idolatrous hearts (Matthew 5:21–28), nor acknowledged the paradoxical and lifetime path of sanctification.

In order to minister effectively to hurting people, the recovery movement reframed the problem and the solution into a parallel gospel, Bible, and church; one that did not shame with self-righteousness; one that did not offer cheap, quick, abstract, impractical solutions; one that did not live with pretense and hypocrisy. But to accomplish its mission it made it easier to

> In attempting to reform the church, the recovery movement has provided an alternative definition of what is wrong, what must happen to change, and how to remain in fellowship with God and others.

face shame by seeing it primarily as the result of a dysfunctional family, it offered a difficult but do-able path by making sanctification a matter of "doing the steps," and it provided a sense of self-worth by teaching people to take care of themselves.

In other words, the recovery movement was a legitimate effort to reform the church, but it has become an alternative that has weakened our view of idolatry, systematized sanctification (in the Twelve Steps), and removed some element of paradox and mystery. The recovery movement has created community on the basis of shared shame in specific addictions rather than on the basis of confessing that each of us is an adulterer and a murderer redeemed by Christ. In attempting to reform the church, the recovery movement has provided an alternative definition of what is wrong, what must happen to change, and how to remain in fellowship with God and others.

## JANICE'S STORY

In recovery Janice owned up to her role in her family. She was the family scapegoat who deflected anger and blame from her parents' marriage to herself. They helped her name the shame she felt and then connected it to her addictive lifestyle. The Twelve Steps helped her begin to organize her internal and external world. Perhaps most of all, recovery gave her a community of caring, honest, struggling people with whom she finally felt free to divulge many secrets that had isolated her from others.

> The soul will not be healed without relationship.

The soul will not be healed without relationship. It was in the context of relationship that we felt most abandoned, violated, and ashamed. It will be in the midst of relationship that we begin to taste the wonder of connection, intimacy, and forgiveness.

The recovery movement offers a rich, passionate connection with a sponsor, a group, and a movement. It is one of the most powerful communities that reflects the priestly love of Jesus. The writer of Hebrews says: "For we do not have a high priest who is unable to sympathize with our weaknesses, but we have one who has been tempted in every way, just as we are—yet was without sin" (Hebrews 4:15).

Who will be this kind of priest? It is a

person who has felt abandoned and knows what it means to be pursued. It will also be a person who knows what it is to abandon and to be invited to join a celebration thrown in the honor of our homecoming. It will be an expert in love. An expert in love is one who studies and pursues the knowledge and experience of intimate relationships. They are students of giving and receiving intimacy, and helping others desire and enter into the wonder of being forgiven.

Janice's recovery group was the first taste of a family who really wanted her to grow. They cared about her life without heavy-handed control or judgment. During this time, Janice ended a number of old relationships and also stopped seeing her parents. She set new boundaries and became both more aware of what she wanted and freer to pursue her desires without guilt.

In retrospect, she said it seemed like she also became more selfish, more defensive, and more presumptuous about what God ought to do. Her desire for safe and nonintrusive friends caused her to end relationships quickly if her needs were not met. If someone said something to her that hurt or offended her, she felt righteous in telling them to back off. Finally, God became an ally in personal healing rather than the holy God to be worshiped.

She remarked: "With the first therapist I never really thought about God even though he was somehow tied in to what we were doing. In the recovery group, he was the one who was giving me the power to do what I needed to do. He was like a banker whom I turned to in order to get me through the tough times. But I never really thought of him as someone to worship. I certainly never thought of my problems as related to my refusal to worship him and instead to turn to gods of my own making. To be honest, during my time in the recovery movement I was never that impressed with being forgiven or Jesus' sacrifice for me. Frankly, it seemed a big deal for sort of a little problem."

Janice to this day is deeply appreciative of the recovery movement. It likely saved her life by enabling her to deal with her alcohol abuse; it also helped her get away from several violent men. But it did

> The route into the gospel is first always bad news.

not take her more deeply into a heart for God and the gospel. The route into the gospel is first always bad news. Bad news involves hearing truth, feeling sorrow and shame. The recovery group is called to speak truth in love, but often it avoids "cross-talk." Cross-talk is any perceived put-down or exposure of fault that may make the person feel bad about himself. The data of relational failure and spiritual indifference is often viewed as off-limits because it may be perceived as shaming or judgmental. As a consequence, relational unity and a shame-free environment often take precedence over struggling together toward the high calling of maturity in Christ.

As a result, the recovery group didn't expose Janice's propensity to move into relationships with manipulative men. There was sufficient data from watching her interact with some of the men in the group, but no one wanted to tangle with her, and so her pattern of seduction and then succumbing to being a victim to the one she seduced was never addressed. Nor did she ever face her core battle with God that was the foundation to her destructive pattern.

Some of the severe patterns of addiction were broken, but there was a spiritual restlessness, a sense that something was missing in her relationship with God. It was when someone invited her to attend a lecture on the relationship between demons and psychological problems that she hoped she might more deeply meet God.

# 12

# Spiritual Interventions: Being Delivered from Evil

JANICE WAS TERRIFIED. Demons. Oppression. Footholds. The words fell from her friend's lips like bombs from the sky. Her friend seemed so casual and confident, but Janice felt sick to her stomach. When her friend asked her if she ever heard voices inside her head, Janice looked straight ahead and said, "Not for some time, but every once in a while."

Her friend smiled and said, "Pretty good indication you are under assault." She asked, "Do you ever feel out of control, like when you are eating ice cream, and you don't want to keep eating but something inside you says go ahead and you do so, and then you feel like dirt for hours?"

Again, Janice's head nodded in silent, distressed assent.

Her friend said: "Pretty good indication some demonic force has a foothold in your heart. I think you will find the lecture tonight very interesting."

Janice did find the lecture both disturbing and reassuring. She learned from the speaker that Satan prowls about the earth to deceive and destroy Christians, but he is no match for God; he is no match for Christians if they simply know his wiles and how to dislodge his current power and protect against future assaults. Most important to Janice, after the lecture and some interaction with the speaker, she found her heart drawn to the mystery and the passion of the real battle: dark powers and principalities of the air, not mere flesh and blood.

She felt like she was finally getting down to business. Counseling had either focused on her past or on her needs and addictions. It seemed so earth-bound, horizontal, and relational. This finally seemed supernatural. She felt a stronger desire to know God and his path for securing safety and freedom.

Soon Janice was reading popular Christian fiction and self-help deliverance books that helped her see the futility of human psychology and how one can be deceived to believe that Satan can not enter and rule the Christian heart. After a few months of reading and talking with friends at church, she sought out a therapist who specializes in combining deliverance, Bible teaching, and counseling. His work with her focused on three issues: (1) discerning satanic footholds and strongholds, (2) deliverance through a truth or power encounter with indwelling demonic forces, and (3) binding evil through spiritual discipline.

*Spiritual intervention models assume that evil inhabits a section of the heart even after conversion.*

169

# SATANIC FOOTHOLDS AND STRONGHOLDS

Spiritual intervention models assume that evil inhabits a section of the heart even after conversion. Evil is like a well-entrenched army that has secret hideaways, caves, and underground passages on the island of the heart. The forces of the kingdom of God may land on the island and truly take possession of the heart for eternity, but eighty-five percent of all Christians have some demonic influence that casts a dark shadow over the soul.

> Footholds in the heart are primarily gained through sexual immorality and unforgiveness.

A "foothold" is a plot of ground in the heart that remains under the control of evil. Paul says in Ephesians 4:26–27, "In your anger do not sin: Do not let the sun go down while you are still angry, and do not give the devil a foothold." Footholds are access points of sin that give evil the capacity to enter the "being" of a person and exert hidden influence over the physical, spiritual, and relational dimensions of life.

Footholds in the heart are primarily gained through sexual immorality and unforgiveness. Past sexual sins open the heart to a "bonding" with evil. When we are unforgiving, the bitterness in the heart permits evil easier access. As well, the practice of habitual sins, past occult practice, and sins of our ancestors may open our heart unwittingly to evil. Even the sins of others, like sexual abuse, can serve as a road evil uses to enter our heart.

A foothold is viewed not as a metaphor of influence but as an actual site in the soul. The Christian is infiltrated by "squatters in the soul"[1] who are an actual "pocket of alien inhabitation within the personality."[2] If these areas are not rooted out, over time they will turn into strongholds that can radically control the person. Evidence of a stronghold is the inability to break a pattern of habitual sin and unbidden negative thoughts against oneself and/or God. Almost any chronic and/or severe symptom is likely the result of an alien, evil being.

The practitioner of spiritual intervention usually assists the sufferer by ascertaining the presence of demonic forces, their access points in the past, and the symptoms of their activity. A "truth" oriented practitioner surveys the person's past immorality, unforgiven sins, or bitterness harbored against others as well as occult history, sexual abuse, and other access points. Some "power" oriented interventions include discovering the demonic names, rank, and number, for it is believed that once the demons are named, they can be evicted.

When Janice went to Dr. Martin for spiritual intervention, she poured out her history over a number of appointments. She was invited to account for every sexual encounter either abusive or immoral. In each case, she was invited to renounce evil's entrance point and confess her need for forgiveness.

> Dr. Martin: Janice, I want you to ask the Spirit of God to recall to your mind another time of sexual sin that was followed by severe self-loathing and other manifestations of demonic activity.
>
> Janice: I guess, you mean where I sort of lost myself in destructive behavior?
>
> Dr. Martin: Yes, but also where uncanny

coincidences or direct manifestations of the demonic occurred like feeling nauseous, or dizzy, or hearing voices.

Janice: Well, I dated one guy who was into pentagrams and stuff like that. Sometimes after sex I felt a spooky presence in the room, and once I felt like the room was moving around me. I may have been drunk, but it was different than just feeling out of control.

Dr. Martin: Janice, you were in the presence of evil, and it likely entered you through the sexual involvement with that man. The manifestation of dizziness, feeling out of control, and certainly the self-hatred is a clear sign of a foothold in your heart.

Janice: (*crying*) I just don't know what to do. I feel sick. I want to vomit. I hated him, but I felt so drawn to him. For days after sex I felt so dirty and cheap. I just can't go on like this.

Dr. Martin: Janice, you can renounce the doorway Satan used to enter your heart. You can confess to God your need for forgiveness and your desire for him to free you from this bondage.

A foothold/stronghold must be exposed, or the Christian will inevitably be defeated. The key to the exposure is locating the demonic influence and its entry point. Most practitioners will not allow a person to say: "The devil made me do it." We are responsible for our lives, but the specific failure to stop masturbating, overeating, or hating ourselves is viewed as a manifestation of demonic handiwork. We are responsible to discover the subtle, intricate hiding places of evil. We are responsible for the individual sin, but the real problem is not the sin behavior, but the driving force behind it. The real problem is demonic—not suppression of the truth, not a willful pursuit of gods of our own making, and not a refusal to repent.

Our true part of responsibility is to face where we left the door unlocked and allowed evil to enter unbidden into our lives. There are two kinds of entry: (1) direct solicitation by turning the heart over to evil, and

(2) indirect, unknown contagion due to the sin of others or the sins of the self. The second is most biblically questionable.

The second view of demonic control enables the sufferer to externalize sin while still owning a more impersonal, disease-like view of one's struggles. I did wrong, but there is a reason—it is not due to my heart's intention; it is a result of an undesired personality within me that sneaked through a window that I should have closed, but did not. In that sense, I am not responsible for my cold, even though I should have more consistently washed my hands. Certainly I am responsible for seeking the proper

It is foolish to minimize the work of Satan. He prowls and seeks to destroy all of humanity. He lies, deceives, and accuses us daily through his horde of diabolical servants.

treatment and joining the process to get well.

It is foolish to minimize the work of Satan. He prowls and seeks to destroy all of humanity. He lies, deceives, and accuses us daily through his horde of diabolical servants. But should we compare his work to a disease that has infiltrated us and now works to mutate the healthy cells into a cancerous mass? Or should we see him as a seducer who pounces on soul weaknesses and whispers—sometimes shouts—invitations to turn from repentance and faith to self-trust?

People who believe in spiritual intervention see the devil as a cancer, and for them the only cure is a truth and/or power encounter with the evil forces that cohabit the heart by someone who is trained in spiritual warfare and deliverance.

## DELIVERANCE THROUGH A TRUTH OR POWER ENCOUNTER

Spiritual intervention requires a climactic, crisis moment of expulsion. If someone exists within us that periodically exerts control over our thoughts and behavior, then it must be removed if the bondage is ever to be broken. The expulsion may involve "power"; that is, the deliverance therapist directly orders evil to name itself, and then banishes it by commands in the name and blood of Christ. A "power" oriented deliverance specialist might say to Janice: "In the name of Christ, I command you demon of addiction to come out and be gone. Release her and never return."

Or the intervention may be a "truth" encounter where the demonic force is not directly commanded to leave, but the person who is inhabited by an evil presence confesses his sin, renounces the presence of evil, and then is cleansed of evil's indwelling power.

In either case, the deliverance therapist surgically cuts away the cancerlike demon through the power of the Holy Spirit. It is the experience and expertise of the deliverance therapist in spiritual warfare that brings the demonic presence to the surface and exposes its hidden foothold/strongholds, then bids it to depart through direct command or an invitation to the sufferer to renounce its presence.

Dr. Martin: Janice, you no longer need to give evil its place in you. Through the Holy Spirit, you can clean house. You can cast out the evil force within you that has driven you to hate yourself and continue in all sorts of destructive eating and masturbation.

Janice: I want to do so.

Dr. Martin: Janice, pray with me. Evil presence that has caused Janice to seal a portion of her heart from God, I command you to release her. In the name of Christ, I forbid you to remain in her and command you in the precious blood of Jesus to relinquish her. (*Janice is sobbing and groaning.*) Janice, I want you to renounce the evil that is about to depart from you.

Janice: I hate you, evil one. I don't want you in me, and I don't want you to ever come back. I renounce the bitterness of my heart toward those who used me and violated me sexually. I confess all the entry ways that have been open to evil, and I close them. I command you evil to leave me now. (*Janice slumps in the chair; she continues quietly to cry.*)

Dr. Martin: Janice, you are free. Evil no longer has a hold of your heart. You are a clean, beautiful, and free daughter of God.

Spiritual deliverance can be dramatic, with demonic forces screaming or pleading to frighten both the victim and the deliverer(s). Or it might be a profound emotional catharsis that enables the victim to draw the line against evil and turn to the soothing balm of forgiveness. In either case, victims of satanic presence report an immediate breakthrough in long-suffered ailments, symptoms, and relational struggles. Where demonic apparitions and unexplained physical happenings used to occur, they no longer do. The person is free.

The allure of freedom from alien thoughts and deeply rooted behaviors that have not responded to willpower or other spiritual disciplines is beyond comprehension. Janice sought therapy and went through countless recovery groups to find relief from her chronic masturbation and her attraction to seductive, destructive men; nothing freed her from the bondage. Over time she lost significant hope that she would ever change. Her first sense of hope came in finding out her problem was an evil presence in her rather than merely her own sin. But the moment evil was cast out of her she felt a profound hope that she had never experienced before.

Her deliverance opened her eyes to the great drama of warfare that was engulfing her. She saw the beguiling evil that was the cause of her self-pity, self-hatred, sexual sin, and relational bondage. Her expulsion of evil enabled her to start with a clean slate and then draw the line to bind evil through newly developed spiritual discipline.

## BINDING EVIL THROUGH SPIRITUAL DISCIPLINE

Spiritual intervention begins with the diagnosis of evil, moves to expulsion, and then strengthens the sufferer to bind evil through spiritual discipline. The notion of binding evil arises from Matthew 12:29. Jesus says: "Or again, how can anyone enter a strong man's house and carry off his possessions unless he first ties up the strong man? Then he can rob his house." We are to bind, tie up the strong man, Satan, by resisting him (James 4:7, 1 Peter 5:9). We are to fight against evil by putting on the whole armor of God (Ephesians 6:10–18).

The spiritual binding of evil involves sensing temptation, rebuking the devil, and then resisting evil's pull, while putting on all the protection and carrying the armaments that we are given to biblically defend ourselves. It may include confessing our sins to our friends, our spiritual director, or our deliverance therapist. It may be necessary under intense, direct assault to be anointed with oil and to have a group of spiritual men and women pray and lay on hands for deliverance.

> **The spiritual binding of evil involves sensing temptation, rebuking the devil, and then resisting evil's pull.**

This component of the deliverance work is most consistent with age-old practices of fighting against evil. It is this kind of exercise that has been classically called spiritual warfare and promoted by books like Bunyan's *Pilgrim's Progress*. But if a prolonged and unrelenting struggle of self-condemnation, habitual sin, or hearing voices returns, then modern spiritual warfare enthusiasts assume new demons have reentered the soul, or a demon that was unseen before has finally come to the surface. The process goes on again and again until greater freedom and strength is gained to fully bind evil.

Dr. Martin: Janice, you must develop the skills to do battle against evil's assaults.

Janice: Well, I am praying more and more and reading the Bible like I never did before.

Dr. Martin: Great. That is very, very important, but you have to have more direct weapons. When you feel temptation, you have to directly rebuke evil and then resist it.

Janice: How do I do that?

Dr. Martin: You need to learn direct deliverance prayers and commands. You need to start by reminding yourself you are a child of God, pure and sinless. Then you need to know the demons that are trying to tempt you. Call them by name. Demons of non-acceptance. Demons of sexual fantasies. I rebuke you in the name of Jesus. Then you need to pray to the Holy Spirit to cover you with his protection. I personally find it helpful to have several Scriptures that mean a great deal to me written out on a three by five card, then I read it to myself until the temptation or conflict begins to subside. You will find that over time just like building physical muscles, the spiritual muscles of resisting the devil will grow, and the battle will usually get easier and easier. When it doesn't, then we have other ways to bind him.

Janice: I am excited. I feel like I can do that with the help of the Holy Spirit. I never realized I was involved in such a monumental battle.

## JANICE'S STORY

Janice dramatically changed through her work with a deliverance therapist. She attended many seminars, read countless books, and turned the corner to a more spiritual life. She told me there were three great truths she learned: (1) she has an enemy of her soul, (2) she is involved daily in the drama of a great war, and (3) she is neither alone, nor resourceless because Jesus is her lover and friend.

In ways that neither dynamic therapy nor her recovery experience ever stated, Janice has unseen, powerful spiritual beings opposed to her life. In the smallest of life concerns, there is a force opposed to her success, health, and intimacy with others. She became sensitized to the wiles of the devil, the hater of her soul, and she began to see life as neither daily, nor ordinary, but as eternal and dramatic.

She no longer saw her hunger to over-eat as merely an effort to fill her empty heart; nor did she recall her past sexual history as simply the shameful outworking of past sexual abuse, nor as an escape from her father's solicitous, confusing involvement. She saw the ordinary and the strange; the past hurts and the psychological struggles as the stage for demonic infiltration and assault. She could now counter his wiles with the weapons of righteousness. She was a warrior for God—brave, bold, knowledgeable, and most important of all, victorious.

But that changed. She eventually faced something that was simple, obvious, and deeply disconcerting to any soul made alive to God's purposes: She did not love well. It may seem unlikely, but one of the most distressing events of her life occurred several years after feeling free of the demonic forces in her life.

She had been involved in the deliverance ministry of her church. She had been used in helping others pray and fight for freedom. Her own life showed continued freedom from the addictions, self-pity, self-hatred, and destructive relationships. She would have said her soul

*She had made the classic error of this culture: Demanding heaven now through some methodology or some person.*

was healed, but a good friend of hers, whom she had helped deliver and disciple, read a book that changed her life.

Janice had once looked at the book and found it too psychological and too hard to read. She had put it aside as a weak sister to the deliverance approach to change. But her friend was deeply moved and drawn to God through this supposedly less truthful, less helpful approach to God. Janice was furious. She felt hurt, misunderstood, and oddly threatened. All her efforts to bind the devil—to thwart his accusations and resist his temptation to doubt and confusion, did not lead her out of pain. She struggled for weeks with no relief.

After many sleepless nights she felt the Spirit of God return her in memory to 1 Corinthians 13—the love chapter. She read it, then began to weep. Inside, she ached more deeply than she had ever done even during her first days of deliverance, for she saw the simple truth: She had made an idol of her approach to God.

How could something so good and so helpful to her life become a path that she demanded others follow? She had become an arrogant follower of an approach, a technique of change. She was so indebted to the man who had taught her how to become free that she resented any other teacher who did not follow her mentor. She had become a Pharisee who followed method and model like an invariant set of rules that had become more important than the God she worshiped.

She had made the classic error of this culture: Demanding heaven now through some methodology or some person. Humbled and drawn back to the utter, simple wonder of being forgiven, she began to rethink her core problem: She was an idol-making factory.

Janice was led into battle by the deliverance approach. She came to understand the kingly lordship of Christ and learned to take his weapons into the battle for his kingdom. In ways that freed her soul, she began to devote her life to reading the Word, praying, fasting, and attending church. But she neglected an honest, probing reflection of her real problem: idolatry. Unwittingly, she became enmeshed in a shallow view of sin; therefore the wonder of forgiveness was not the basis of daily growth in faith, hope, and love.

The deliverance approach brought Janice to a clear, simple understanding of her true

> **True soul care never ignores or denies either the horizontal or the vertical dimensions of life—both open the heart to facing and embracing our daily ache to know Jesus as the forgiving, passionate pursuer of our soul.**

enemy and the need for spiritual growth. But in seeing the struggle of life in light of demonic forces, she forgot the importance of her story, her past, and the influence of flesh and blood people in her life. She became so vertically-minded, she lost sight of the power and importance of the horizontal in shaping her life for good or ill. Many deliverance therapists minimize the importance of understanding and grappling with the past as the raw material Satan uses to deceive, lie, and accuse the soul through the whispering seduction to trust in gods other than God. True soul care never ignores or denies either the horizontal or the vertical dimensions of life—both open the heart to facing and embracing our daily ache to know Jesus as the forgiving, passionate pursuer of our soul.

## TRUE SOUL CARE

The soul is healed not merely through more insight (dynamic therapy), deeper connection and shame-free encouragement (recovery therapy), or in greater deliverance from evil (spiritual intervention). The soul is healed as we grow in faith, hope, and love through prophetic truth, priestly community, and a kingly movement into the war of love.

It was my privilege to work with Janice in counseling. Her work in considering her past, her addictions, and the influence of the demonic needed to be neither substantially challenged, nor debated. I differ considerably with many aspects of each approach, but the heart of what each model attempts to accomplish is not inconsistent with a biblical approach to change and recovering hope for life.

My counseling invited her to take each approach further as she more deeply considered her past in light of her search to find a more predictable god than God. She struggled to know a shame-free connection that did not minimize the high call of growing in maturity. We also looked more closely at how evil had attempted to use the past abuse to destroy faith, hope, and love. I am neither so foolish, nor arrogant to believe my work was all she needs to pursue maturity. But she grew another few feet in the long journey of becoming like Christ.

She grew to know Jesus Christ as the prophet of her soul that disrupts her suppression of truth and offers her hope. She found he is also the priest of her soul that has felt all her infirmities and emotions, but who is without sin and who connects her to the Father through faith. He is her king who leads her into the battle of life with the weapons of love for the purpose of love. In chapter 14, I will explore more thoroughly these roles of prophet, priest, and king and what they mean in the context of finding hope for healing.

# PART
# 4

# What Can I
# Hope For?

# 13

# Shepherds and Specialists: Resources for Help

 ⤫ 

WITHOUT THE HOPE OF heaven we Christians are a miserable lot. We're banking on tomorrow to be better than today. That's why we're willing to put up with suffering now without making it our ultimate business to relieve it.

So what can we hope for today, in the middle of eating disorders, memories of abuse, strained marriages, rebellious kids, panic attacks, and feelings about ourselves and our lives that we just don't like? Does the gospel take away all the suffering? Some of it? None of it? Does it help us endure what God won't improve till heaven?

If we get serious about finding help when we're hurting, what can we expect? Let me tell a story to illustrate two common approaches people take when they seek help, approaches that create very different expectations.

## MOVING THE COUCH INTO THE CHURCH

It was only my second radio interview, for this was in the early stages of my career, over twenty years ago. The host of the weekly religious talk show, a pastor in Miami, had read an article of mine in *Christianity Today* magazine entitled "Moving the Couch into the Church." In that article, I suggested what has since become a theme in my thinking, that the local church could do more to meet the counseling needs of its people, that it might be wrong to routinely refer folks with personal concerns to professional therapists when natural community, if it functioned properly, could more powerfully address those same concerns.

The pastor was intrigued. He invited me to discuss my ideas on his radio show. I don't have a transcript of the interview, but the first few minutes went something like this:

Host: "Dr. Crabb, isn't it unusual for you, a trained psychologist, to tell people to cancel their appointments with their Christian counselors and talk to their pastor instead, or maybe sign up for a support group in their church?"

Guest: "That's not exactly what I'm suggesting, but I do believe the church has unique resources for ministering to troubled people that are not being fully used."

Host: "And I agree with you. I've pastored now for more than thirty years and I've seen literally hundreds, probably thousands, of hurting people find deep encouragement within the church community. We've been careful, of course, to refer those who have real psychological problems to competent professionals. But you're right. The church needs to be—and can be—a source of rich encouragement to its members."

Guest: "I think it can do more than that. I'm wondering if mature Christians can't do the same kind of good that therapists do in their offices. I know what goes on in therapy sessions, and much of it is good. People talk about deep issues of the soul and what it means to know Christ's love through all the ups and downs of life. And that's true psychotherapy, the care and cure of the soul. But isn't that the job of the church? Why can't that be done by pastors and elders and other godly Christians? My point is . . ."

Host: "Well, let me tell you how I see things. When I counsel with a person from my church, the first thing I do is check to see if I'm in over my head. I can deal with spiritual matters and some of the problems people get into in their relationships and so on, but if they have a psychological problem, if something is deep-seated, then I urge them to see one of the three or four Christian therapists I've learned to trust."

Guest: "But . . ."

Host: "It's no different than when I visit church members in the hospital who are about to have surgery. You wouldn't expect me to deal with that one, would you? I have a word of prayer, then I walk alongside as they're wheeled down the hallway. But when we reach the operating theater, I stay outside while the surgeon goes in to do what he's trained to do. But I wait right there in the hallway and I tell my parishioners that's where I'll be— and I pray till the doctor comes out. I feel the same way when I send someone to see a good psychologist, like you. I can pray, but you're trained to do the therapy."

About then, as I recall, I gave up trying to make my point.

## THE TWO SIDES

People today line up on one side or the other on this issue of the place of therapy in the church. The great majority agree with my radio host. They believe that family, friends, and pastors have an important role to play in helping people live fulfilling, godly lives. But if they have real problems, that role becomes largely supportive, something like a water boy's role at a football game. If the quarterback is thirsty, send in the water boy. But if he breaks his arm, call the orthopedic surgeon. Natural community (the water boy) provides encouragement. But when something comes apart in your life, ask your pastor to pray as you drive to the counseling center. After all, you need more than encouragement to deal with the deeper issues. You need a trained specialist, such as a therapist, psychiatrist, recovery expert, or certified biblical counselor.

On the other side of the issue is a small but vocal minority. They don't believe there is such a thing as a "diseased psyche." They think that psychological problems are really spiritual problems, that pastors and elders are equipped by their calling and biblical knowledge to do whatever needs doing to restore people to godly living. They're not mere water boys. They're spiritual surgeons, fully equipped to deal not with a diseased psyche but with a sinful soul. In their view, pastors can do more than pray in the hallway while the therapist does the work. They should charge into the "operating" room, tell the therapist to leave, then pray, teach, admonish, expose, and support until the patient stands up and walks out in newness of life.

Christian culture lives in tension between these two options: (1) call in the professional when the problems are severe, and (2) let the pastor do it all. Those who argue either way have no difficulty coming up with horror stories to buttress their position. "My daughter went to a therapist and now believes that her father abused her when she was little. Since that repressed memory came back in therapy, she'll have nothing to do with any of her family. I believe the memory is false, but even if it's true, she should be working toward forgiveness and reconciliation."

Or, on the other side, "I told my pastor that I was struggling with lust. He immediately told me to confess it as sin, memorize several Bible verses, and pray until God gave me victory. The whole session lasted maybe ten minutes. I never felt so judged or unhelped in all my life."

Most people, whether in the professional community or the church, subscribe to the philosophy of the radio pastor, that family, friends, and pastors are helpful, but only to a point. When that point is reached, someone with more training must take over. The water boy must watch helplessly as the ambulance whisks away the broken-armed quarterback to the hospital. The trained specialist might be a therapist, physician, recovery expert, certified biblical counselor, or a graduate of the church's lay counselor training program, but he or she must have more knowledge and skill than the average family member, friend, or pastor.

## WATER BOYS

Let's go back to our answer to the question, "What's wrong with me?" As I look over the six possible explanations for our problems, I am struck by the fact that none of them would direct us to natural community as our primary resource for finding healing.

If the explanation for our problem is **spiritual warfare**, we turn to resources found only in God, perhaps mediated by specialists who understand the tactics of spiritual warfare.

If the explanation is **dysfunctional background**, then the problem is likely psychological, and we need a trained counselor.

If the explanation is either **personal sin** or **undisciplined living**, the resources God has already placed within us should be sufficient. Biblical counselors might help and church community can hold us accountable, but the primary resource is our will.

If the explanation is **biochemical disorder**, medical personnel are necessary.

If the explanation is **deficient spirituality**, then God, ourselves, and perhaps a spiritual director should be able to improve things (and the trend is toward requiring special training in order to claim the title "Spiritual Director").

In every case, natural community is reduced to the role of water boy. In no case are family, friends, or pastors considered the most valued resource in dealing with personal problems, and certainly they are never a sufficient resource unless the problem is considered to be minor.

# PATTY AND PAUL

Patty leads a support group in her church. Although she has a master's degree in counseling, she presents herself to the group more as a friend and Bible teacher. Most members aren't aware of her counseling degree.

In her role as a shepherd, she encourages the women to "tell their stories," to share their personal struggles with the group. But when an especially difficult story is told, a member of the group (who has made sure everyone knows that she is a licensed counselor) typically says, "You might want to consider getting professional help. Your problem could be pretty deep." The message is clear: this group can provide enough water to slake your thirst, but you may need real help.

Paul had been a good friend of Leon's for a long time. Since college days, when Leon was an assistant dean of men during Paul's freshman year, Paul had looked to Leon as a big brother. Now, years later, Paul was thirty— and single. He had talked to Leon, now thirty-nine and married with three kids, about his fear of commitment and how badly his knees shook whenever a relationship with an eligible young woman took a serious turn.

The talks were always friend to friend,

usually over lunch, sometimes in Leon's home with his wife joining in. Then it happened. Strengthened by Leon's encouragement, Paul took the plunge. He asked Annette to marry him. For the next several months, the engaged couple spent hours with Leon and his wife, discussing everything from personal histories and present anxieties to kids, in-laws, and sex.

During one conversation over lunch, Paul said to Leon, "You know, I was thinking. Maybe before Annette and I get married, we should get some premarital counseling. What do you think of . . ." and he mentioned a recently licensed counselor who was twenty-eight years old and single.

## OFFICE VERSUS LIVING ROOM

We can't get it out of our heads that what happens in a professional's office is necessarily different—deeper, more helpful—than what happens with a wise friend in his living room. People in natural community provide encouragement, maybe a little advice, a few good biblical reminders, and some meaningful prayer; but trained people in professional community offer therapy, a unique kind of conversation that goes much deeper and does more good. That's what we think.

Is it possible that our idea of encouragement is too weak? Could profound listening release rich wisdom in Spirit-dependent Christians that might transform natural community into a powerful vehicle for changing lives?

I'm familiar with the disappointment of many people who have turned to friends and pastors for help. I know a few pastors who bash people with the Bible or pompously deliver a few platitudes to deeply wounded folks that only increases their pain. I know some elders who play amateur therapist and stir up storms they have no idea how to calm. I know many elders who manage people the way they manage church business, with a few good principles and a warm word of encouragement. And I know scores of well-meaning friends who deeply care but haven't a clue what to tell parents whose teenagers are sleeping around or taking drugs.

The truth is that people who turn to natural community for help usually come away frustrated. Unless, of course, their problems require nothing more than a cup of cold water. That's the way it is.

But we assume that the way it is, is the way it must be. Real problems, we think, need help that only specialists can provide.

For a moment, consider another line of thought. Suppose community has been functioning way below its potential for years. Suppose the water in our bucket has healing properties we can't imagine—and therefore we haven't bothered to run on the field when the player is injured. Suppose that what we moderns call community bears little resemblance to the real thing. Then, it would be a very good idea to do everything we can to recover true community and pass the bucket around to everybody.

Until we experience a taste of what natural community can provide through family, friends, and spiritual leaders, we'll stay on the sidelines with our water buckets when someone really needs help. What can community provide? What *is* community? Is there something about the nature of our personal problems that makes community the ideal context for dealing with them?

In a day when community (particularly the local church) has too often yielded its soul-curing role to specialists who do most of their work outside community, two questions deserve special attention:

1. Could family, friends, and spiritual leaders somehow be released to do

more good than anyone now imagines?

2. If so, how do we go about releasing them?

With a burden to see the work of healing souls restored to ongoing natural community, I take up these questions in chapter 15. I want to see the day when struggling people turn to their church communities for the help they need—and find it. I want to see the day when the local church—not the weekend seminar, the Christian counseling center, or the private therapist's office—is thought of as the place where the really important things take place, things like the healing and restoration of troubled souls.

But that day is not now and may not come for many years. For at least that reason, there is still a good and honorable place for professional counseling in our society. Before I sketch my dream of what community could provide for its members, even those with "real" problems, Dan Allender makes the case for the Christian professional, suggesting in the next chapter what I believe as well, that trained counselors have a legitimate role to play in healing the souls of struggling Christians.

# 14

# The Special Gift of a Christian Counselor

❦

A GOOD COUNSELOR IS both uniquely gifted and trained to offer others a taste of Jesus Christ. A godly counselor is first of all a man or woman who is committed far less to a particular model, style, or approach to counseling than to representing Christ in all he or she does with others.

A counselor's greatest gift to a client is offering him or her a vision of Christ as our prophet who exposes our heart and engenders hope; our priest who enters our struggles and deepens our faith by reminding us in word and deed of Christ's sacrifice on our behalf; and our king who leads

206

us into battle utilizing the weapons of love to fight for his kingdom. A godly counselor is gifted in making Christ known in the trenches of inner battles and interpersonal struggles.

But are we not all to be counselors according to this perspective? Of course, we are. Every person who knows Jesus Christ is to make him known as a prophet, priest, and king. It is called the "general" calling. But for centuries there has been a distinction made between general and special calling. Everyone is called to be involved in the work of God, but some are specially called to give their lives and their gifts to a specific expertise to enhance the body of Christ.

## THE NEED FOR SPECIALISTS

Sadly we live in an era where there is a growing animosity toward specialists or experts because they seem to replace those with general gifts for service. In the area of counseling, the division between special gifts and training and the more general people-helping gifts are the basis of a growing schism that is not necessary if we understand the role of counseling in the body of Christ and the difference between general and special gifts.

For example, we are called to worship God in song, praise, and prayer. No question some are uniquely gifted to lead others in worship. I have been led in worship by some who are well-meaning, but untrained and of average gift. Worship, like all of life, is not dependent on another person's gifts, or absence of them, but it is more difficult to worship when incompetence, inexperience, or untrained enthusiasm gets in the way. On the other hand, I have preached in churches where a man or woman who is musically gifted, prepared, and committed has structured the music to fit the message and has orchestrated the singers and musicians to play at their best—the result was incomprehensible. I am delighted that some are uniquely called to lead public prayer, plan worship services, and utilize

> A counselor's greatest gift to a client is offering him or her a vision of Christ as our prophet, priest, and king.

their gifts for the larger body of Christ. I feel the same about counselors.

Just as there is a place for pastors, administrators, worship leaders, teachers, and theologians, so there is a place in the body of Christ for trained and financially compensated counselors. And not merely as a concession to the body of Christ not doing its work of caring for others.

The rise of therapy may be sadly connected to the self-righteousness and superficiality of many in the body of Christ, but the ministry of reflection, soul-searching, and soul care should not be solely left as a general calling—to grow in competence and skill there must be some who follow the special

Sadly we live in an era where there is a growing animosity toward specialists or experts because they seem to replace those with general gifts for service.

calling through training, supervision, and licensure.

To assume godly men and women in general are to do the bulk of the work of teaching, counseling, and leading the body of Christ is to deny special giftedness and unique training. To presume we are all equally called to the same tasks is not only a misguided egalitarian view of gifts, but it is an attempt to democratize calling and require everyone to be the same in the body of Christ. I am not a singer. I am not gifted at worship. But I am gifted as a teacher and a counselor. I am eternally grateful for my seminary and counseling graduate school education. I would not be the person I am without it. Therefore, I am radically committed to education and to the enhancement of special gifts in these areas without in any way ignoring or denigrating the "general" call for all Christians to pursue the knowledge and expertise of pastor, teacher, counselor, worship leader, theologian, etc.

The counselor, like all mature believers, is trained to live out in his sphere the integrity, the uniqueness of Christ. Specifically, the trained and professionally oriented therapist is more of a prophet than a priest or king. But if the therapist is growing in

210

Christ, then in all areas of practice and life, he represents the fullness of Christ as a priest and a king.

## Peggy and John

Godly therapists do not merely offer professional services in a private practice setting; they live out their gifts and training in all the dimensions of life. For example, recently I had lunch with two hurting friends. By sharing our conversation with you, I have chosen to illustrate what I believe is the core of all good therapy (and by implication what is needed to heal the soul). What I did as friend was informed and guided by my work and training as a therapist. I served two hurting friends as a prophet, priest, and king, but primarily as a prophet.

The lunch had been served and the waitress quickly asked the standard question: "Is there anything else I can get you?" She must have noticed an uncomfortable tension hanging over the table because she started to move away even before an answer could be offered.

Peggy and John, good friends, sat quietly waiting for her to depart. Peggy's eyes were cloudy from days of crying; John was stiff and defensive. He was awaiting either another deluge from Peggy or the expected confrontation he had heard from other friends that had met with them.

John had made his intention known—he was leaving Peggy. He could not endure the emptiness, hypocrisy, and confusion he felt in living a Christian life when he no longer considered himself to be a Christian. At least not a Christian who took Christ seriously. He had come to the end of the game, and he knew what he was doing was wrong, but he had no intention of changing his mind.

The meal had been set up by Peggy. Prior to our lunch I heard her pour out her fear and confusion, hurt and anger. She was desperate and asked if I would be willing to meet with them. I agreed. But I was confused. What did she expect me to accomplish? John had already met with several elders from the church. They had questioned, pled, and confronted him, but to no avail. Several weeks had passed, and though he had not moved out, it was clear he was progressing toward separation.

I knew it was pointless to cover the same terrain already well stated by the elders—John knew he was sinning. He had heard from well-meaning friends that he was going through a mid-life crisis—he knew he was

confused. He had been questioned by many—
he knew what to expect. He had been threatened, consoled, and tears had been shed on
his behalf by many. As I sipped my soda, I
again asked God to give me words that might
be used at some point to provoke curiosity,
to point toward the God who had won his
heart, and to provide a path for more than
mere restoration of his marriage, but for radical change of his heart.

Dan: John, Peggy called me a few
days ago, so I know a little
about the situation. I know
you've talked with some of
the men from church. Tell me
why you've agreed to have
lunch with me given the fact
that you know or suspect what
I am going to say?

John: Well, I guess to make it a little
bit easier for Peg. I know I
have hurt her deeply, but there
is nothing left to talk about.
I care for her and want her to
be happy, but I don't love
her—I don't think I have for
years, and I can't stay in this
marriage when it's dead. I

can't pretend that I am a Christian or that it matters to me what God thinks. I think it will be better for us both if we can get beyond this tough time and start our lives over again.

Peggy: I don't know how you can say that, John. We have been married nearly twenty-three years, and, yes, there have been problems, but you have never been willing to talk about them. And now you're calling it quits when we haven't even talked to a counselor or anyone about our marriage.

John: Peggy, I am sorry. You may be right, but it's too late . . .

Peggy: It's never too late. You know that. There is no reason we can't get through this if we just trust in the Lord.

Dan: Peggy, let me cut you off for a moment to clarify a few things. John, it's clear you agreed to this lunch to be kind to Peggy and to satisfy her request. Is that accurate?

John: Yes.

Dan: Then let me state the obvious. You don't want to wrestle with the issues that have ruined your marriage. You don't want my input, my confrontation, or my sorrow. If I am wrong, tell me, but if not, then is there anything you want from me?

John: I hope you can help Peggy see that it is best that we just move on and do so in the best way for each other and the kids.

Dan: I would be willing to do that.

Peggy: What? Are you saying you agree with him? Are you serious?

Dan: Yes, I am. I see no point in trying to twist John's arm. But give me a moment to clarify what I mean and to ask a few questions. Is that all right with you both?

Both of their heads nodded. John sat forward; for the first time his face relaxed. Peggy sat back, and her despair lifted with the first clear signs of anger.

Dan: John, Peggy said there have been a number of issues that have made your marriage sort of constipated. Accurate?

John: Yeah. I don't know if I would have been willing to admit that before or even use that word, but it fits.

Dan: Don't worry, I am not trying to get you to talk about those issues. But I am assuming that your unwillingness to talk or deal with them indicates some heart not to hurt your wife. The discussions would have been painful for her. But I also assume your unwillingness reflects a typical cowardice. You did not know what to do with the problems, and so you refused to enter the confusion of the situation. Am I in the ballpark?

John: I suppose. Yeah. I mean, I have lived with rules and responsibilities that I have obeyed because I was afraid of what others might think if I chucked them. I won't do that anymore.

Dan: So with regard to Peggy, with others, with God, you've lived a cowardly life, never really asking the tough questions, nor putting words to the war you've ignored inside you.

John: I get your point. You just think I am doing another cowardly thing.

Dan: (*Laughing*) Yup. But again, given the kind of life you lived before, I can't imagine why Peggy would be that thrilled to get you back. I am certainly not saying separation and divorce is a great improvement, but at least you are sick of the silly, thoughtless, godless, cowardly existence you were living before.

Peggy: But at least we were caring for the kids and doing what was right.

Dan: Peggy, I know you are in pain, afraid, and frankly fairly angry with me. But may I speak honestly? Okay. The fact is, your marriage was likely a boring, predictable, moral, self-righteous mess. Again, for your sake, I will say it straight: John is wrong to leave you. Worse, he is a coward. But at least he has chosen not to perpetuate a marriage of form that lacks heart and passion. If he merely came back and said, "Okay, we will work on our sexual relationship, our communication, our distance," would you be happy?

Peggy: Yes, I guess I am willing to settle for very little, but that sounds like a whole lot better than what we have had in the past.

Dan: Right. But it is not much different than saying, "Why don't you all take a trip together and maybe something will get sparked?" It deals with the external; it offers the hope of change, without getting to the heart.

John: Right. That's what you've always wanted. Things to be

better by changing location, getting away, or just pretending there are no problems. I can't take it anymore.

Dan: John, you've not wanted my input. I'll not offer it unless you want me to.

John: What do you want to say?

Dan: Simple, my friend. You are finally a prodigal. Like the older son, you've labored in the back fields but hated the Father for wanting the younger son to return. I don't commend you for your sin, but I do commend you for saying, Enough of pretense and self-righteous drudgery. But do you really want more . . . really? Or do you just want to take your cowardice in a different direction? A change from two-piece suit conformity and cowardice to a radical rebellion that hides your refusal to battle with your wife, with me, with God?

John: No one has ever called me a coward before. I know it's true. But I know I can't go back. I don't want to hurt Peggy, but I know I just don't want to hurt anymore.

Dan: Your option is not pain or no pain. Life will not grant that option. Your option is whether you want to face your hunger or hide out with the pigs for a while. I am so glad you can't go back. It is a mark of integrity. I can help your wife grapple with her sin and her willingness to accept the form of marriage and her refusal to struggle for real intimacy. I will, if she is willing. But it does grieve me you would move this far with integrity to give up the form, but then fall back on cowardice to simply end a marriage that likely never began.

John: I know it sounds abrupt, but I did not expect our time to go this way, and I have more going on inside of me than I want to say now. I don't know what I will do, but I will say I am more disturbed now than I was when we first sat down. I still intend to end this marriage, but I will grant you that there is more to this than I understand. I will get back to you both. I suppose I ought to thank you. Thanks a lot. (*He leaves.*)

Peggy: (*In tears*) I don't know what to say. He seems more troubled than he has been with anyone else. He wrote everyone off quickly. But your direction almost seems to invite him to leave me. I'm so afraid.

The conversation ended, and it took several weeks before John called me back. I have worked with many situations similar to this, and the man has refused to admit his flight was cowardice. I have seen a number of marriages end in divorce, but John was troubled, and he did not bail out of his marriage. He separated from his wife. He began talking regularly to another good friend of mine, an excellent therapist, and he met every now and then with me to reflect on the thoughts that were coming to the surface as a result of the process.

His therapy opened his heart to look at matters that were sufficiently complex and painful that it would have been impossible to enter that domain in a public setting or in hit-and-miss meals. John would report his work with a therapist was life-changing. But it was augmented by my occasional interactions with him at breakfast.

Our times at breakfast were often rambling discourses where each of us reflected on our lives, our understanding of Scripture, and our struggle to know and live out the gospel. John changed. His heart became more tender, more alive, stronger. His relationship with Peggy changed as well.

> **Therapy is no cure; in fact, it can increase the disease of demandingness that originally brought the person to the point of asking for help.**

At first, Peggy was thrilled the marriage did not end, but John's changes began to require her to change more than she had bargained for. As often happens, she wanted the marriage to work and she was open to some change, but when the depths of her sin became clear, she balked, and it was Peggy who almost ended the marriage.

Peggy saw another therapist. For a time her self-righteousness soared, her demands became more self-serving, and her heart hardened. Therapy is no cure; in fact, it can increase the disease of demandingness that originally brought the person to the point of asking for help. In time, after much pain, this couple began to allow their hearts to know God and each other in ways that revolutionized their relationship. They were in love again; more importantly, they began to love each other in ways they had never offered before.

## Disrupted, Connected, Directed

What happened? What happened in the original conversation that opened the door to healing? What occurred in their work in therapy? To answer these questions, let me tell you about a few convictions that I hold about the process of change and growth.

1. People change if they are willing to wrestle with God and with other

human beings about the deep matters of the heart.

2. People change to the degree they are drawn into an intimate relationship with God and other human beings.

3. People change to the degree they obediently walk in the path of the royal law of love based on the wonder of being forgiven.

To change, I desperately need to be disrupted (#1), connected (#2), and directed (#3). What happened with John that opened the door to change? I surprised John. He expected a moral lecture; instead I exposed both his cowardly flight from his wife and his courageous confession that his marriage was dead. John was invited simultaneously to face his sin and to see his integrity in a different light (disruption). I also remained kind, playful, and open to him in spite of his sin (connection). And I was willing to lead, to walk with him toward life if he wanted to move (direction). At a human level those gifts are what the spirit of God uses to change a human heart. The Spirit convicts, teaches, and guides, but he graciously uses us as the context to administer supernatural change.

What we need to offer others is a taste of Jesus Christ. People change to the degree they experience and understand the gospel. The three elements—disruption, connection, and direction—are components of the work of Christ. In theological writing, Christ's earthly ministry is often talked about as fulfilling the roles of a prophet, priest, and king. He is the perfect embodiment of the prophet who disrupts and offers hope; the priest who connects and instills faith; and the king who lovingly, justly leads his people into battle against evil.

Who is a good therapist? It is the one who offers a full picture of Jesus Christ in the way they interact with others. Jesus alone is our mediator, the one who can restore us to relationship with God through his death and resurrection. No one can fulfill his per-

> What we need to offer others is a taste of Jesus Christ. People change to the degree they experience and understand the gospel.

fect meditorial role; but we can disrupt like a prophet, connect like a priest, and lead like a king. The three elements of prophet, priest, and king are lenses to evaluate what a good counselor offers her client.

## Prophetic Disruption

In my conversation with John I had an idea what he expected me to do. He had talked with other Christian leaders and knew enough about the Bible to know he was wrong. But he did not see what he was doing as that wrong because he felt so empty, so tired, and so drawn to the freedom that sin offered. It would have been useless to come against the same defenses that had been reinforced after so many assaults.

The role of a prophet is to surprise, disrupt, and open the door to hope. It is to speak truth in a way that gets the attention of the listener and sneaks into the issues of the soul through the unexpected crack in the heart.

I chose to begin our conversation as a prophet. I took the initiative and asked why he had agreed to the meal given his past conversations with other church leaders and his "expectations" of what I would say. By asking about the issue of his "desire" I put him in the position of talking from his heart rather than defending his choice. I also suspected he was meeting with me to please his wife. Even in ending his marriage, he was a nice, but weak man. I hoped he might be slightly open to seeing his flight as a deepening of the cowardice that had killed his marriage rather than as a solution to the hollowness of his marriage.

A prophet exposes the hardness of the heart and warns and invites the idolatrous heart to return to God. He stands in the way of deceit and pretense. He calls the people to remember God and to reflect on the consequences of continued rebellion. A prophet stands like the child in the midst of the royal procession and states the obvious: the emperor has no clothes.

The role of a prophet is to surprise, disrupt and open the door to hope. It is to speak truth in a way that gets the attention of the listener.

Jeremiah cried out about the priesthood and other prophets:

> "From the least to the greatest, all are greedy for gain; prophets and priests alike, all practice deceit. They dress the wound of my people as though it were not serious. 'Peace, peace,' they say, when there is no peace. Are they ashamed of their loathsome conduct? No, they have no shame at all; they do not even know how to blush. So they will fall among the fallen; they will be brought down when I punish them," says the LORD. (Jeremiah 6:13–15)

Jeremiah, like his fellow prophets, exposed the heart's true motives and focused on the relational/psychological by-products of sin. The leaders refused to blush, to feel shame for their idolatry and the prophet called them to feel, to see, and to change.

But rarely does a prophet simply say: "Here is your sin, now stop it." Instead, through story and drama he finds the right moment and right words to expose the true intentions of the heart. He intensifies choice rather than merely exhorting change.

The prophet is an expert in the ways

of sin, the power of well-timed exposure, and the passion of hope. A glorious example of expertise is Nathan's rebuke of King David, after he had committed adultery with Bathsheba and arranged for Uriah to be killed. Nathan, the prophet, stunned David with his compelling story of a man who owned thousands of sheep, but stole the one sheep owned by a poor farmer. David became so incensed he shouted, "As surely as the Lord lives, the man who did this deserves to die!" Nathan responded, "You are the man!" (2 Samuel 12:1–7). A prophet knows that mere encouragement, support,

A prophet knows that mere encouragement, support, and connection are not enough to change the human heart; we need to be caught, exposed, and surprised in our ways of making life work for us.

and connection are not enough to change the human heart; we need to be caught, exposed, and surprised in our ways of making life work for us.

Why? Sin is both a deeply entrenched barnacle in the soul and also a shifting and subtle vapor. Richard Lovelace, an eminent theologian, writes:

> The structure of sin in the human personality is something far more complicated than the isolated acts and thoughts of deliberate disobedience commonly designated by the Word. In its biblical definition, sin cannot be limited to isolated instances or patterns of wrongdoing; it is something much more akin to the psychological term "complex": an organic network of compulsive attitudes, beliefs, and behavior deeply rooted in our alienation from God. . . . The human heart is now a reservoir of unconscious disordered motivation and response.[1]

The prophet draws forth sin, exposes it, and then offers the hope of repentance and reconciliation with the Father. For that reason, I tried to help Peggy see that if she wanted John back as he was, she was not only compromising herself, but failing to love John. I tried to do that with John by contrasting his past superficial obedience with being the older brother and his current flight from Peggy as equivalent to being the prodigal son. The prodigal ran from the Father. However, the story in Luke 15 is also about the brother who stayed with the Father, but served him out of obligation, not love. Henri Nouwen in his book, *The Return of the Prodigal Son*, notes that we are at times both the prodigal and the older brother. In a sense, John played the prodigal, but only after years of empty, ritualized service as an older brother.

In some sense, John's current sin was preferable to his self-righteous, cowardly service of God and his wife in the back fields. But to leave him with those two options only would be horrible. I wanted him to know that a third option existed. Leave the back fields, of course. But one need not go live with pigs for long before realizing there is a better option: return to the Father. I wanted him to feel the emptiness of being the older brother; the loneliness of being the prodigal; and the joy of coming home. The offer of hope is a key part of our prophetic work.

Prophets speak of sin and destruction, and they also envision a day of righteousness and restoration. The prophet reminds people that God is crazy about them. Isaiah promises: "Yet the LORD longs to be gracious to you; he rises to show you compassion. . . . How gracious he will be when you cry for help! As soon as he hears, he will answer you" (Isaiah 30:18–19).

**Change will not occur without disruption of deceit and blindness. But it will also not occur unless hope is offered as a motivation to change.**

Change will not occur without disruption of deceit and blindness. But it will also not occur unless hope is offered as a motivation to change. And to offer hope is to tap into the heart's deepest desires: the hunger for rest, joy, peace, bounty, and reconciliation. The prophet in that case is a poet of the future—helping enter the hunger that has been denied or hardened and then seeing the path to pursue to taste the desired joy.

## Priestly Connection

If the prophet disturbs, the priest comforts. The prophet looks at horizontal reality in order to drive the heart back to God; the priest looks to God in order to remind the people of his goodness and grace. The priest and prophet ought to be neither in competition, nor in conflict. They are bearers of truth viewed from two different perspectives and tasks. The prophet provokes the heart to repentance, and the priest draws the broken, hungry heart to taste the goodness of God (Psalm 34:6).

My conversation with John and Peggy is possible to transcribe, but almost impossible to replay in mood and texture. How did I feel toward them? How did they experience me in their presence? I recall feeling sad and kind toward them both. I did not feel pressured, worried, or frustrated. I believe they knew that I cared for each of them with no agenda on my part to somehow save the marriage or get one or both of them to change. They knew I cared.

A priest offers his presence as a glimpse of the merciful face of God. In many ways it is impossible to describe how to do it; it is either in your heart toward a person, or it is not. But a true priest sees the person from the eyes of God and knows the privilege of lifting the eyes of the other to look to God.

The priest also speaks words of life. Where a person can be affirmed and encouraged because her heart is like God, then a priest speaks truth. Just as the priestly psalmist declares: "My heart is pure," so can we acknowledge goodness, beauty, integrity wherever we taste it. I did that with John by saying that his integrity at least had taken him to the point of giving up a hollow, self-righteous marriage. I followed that direction by inviting his integrity to grow to the point to cause him to return home.

> The prophet provokes the heart to repentance, and the priest draws the broken, hungry heart to taste the goodness of God.

The priest invites the struggling heart to glimpse the God who rescues his undeserving children from harm. The priest invites and connects the heart to the remembrance of God's faithful acts of redemption in the past.

The task of the priest is to draw the troubled, plowed-up heart into relationship with God. He invites the heart to cry out to God in confusion, anger, hurt, and desire. It is striking to remember that the psalms, the prayer and song book of the temple, is made up of more songs of lament than praise. Walter Bruggemann has said the psalms can be divided between songs of orientation, disorientation, and reorientation. These labels also describe the work of a priest.

> A priest offers his presence as a glimpse of the merciful face of God.

A priest points people to consider God as the core of existence, to be served in all we do (orientation). But life is disturbing, and we struggle with what God is up to. We experience him as silent, or worse, opposed to us. His apparent refusal to save us throws our world into chaos, and a priest leads us in the expression of lament (disorientation). Finally, God does save. He saved in the past, and his purposes will not be thwarted in the present. Salvation leads us to sing songs of thanksgiving (reorientation). A priest is the leader of the celebration.

A priest feels the heartache and struggle of the people. He draws the sinful heart to God, announces the provision of redemption, and invites the forgiven to celebrate. As a teacher of the Word, he orients our heart to the principles of the law; as one who knows the heart, he proclaims our inability to keep the law; and as one who has tasted the grace of God, he proclaims the forgiveness of sin that comes from being marked by the blood of the Lamb.

## Kingly Leadership

The prophet disturbs; the priest comforts; and the king leads. The prophet provokes the heart to face reality, the priest proclaims that God is at the core of all that is real, and the king pronounces how to live in reality. The king leads and protects his people by applying wisdom to the war of life.

A king, in the Old Testament, was the

human analog of what was called the "divine warrior" (Psalm 45).[2] God is our king, and he fights on our side to destroy all that is opposed to him and to provide the context to grow all that is good (Psalm 86). He is a warrior/king who seeks justice and mercy for his people in order to mirror the coming kingdom of righteousness.

A king directs. I offered Peggy the opportunity to deal with her husband on a different plane than she had before. I did not think it wise at that meal to offer to lead John. All I wanted to do was to disturb him and entice him to a new life. But Peggy claimed to want to work on her life and marriage, and I told her I would be willing to help her walk a path toward greater maturity. A king does not assure the resolution of a problem; he only offers to lead a person in the path of maturity.

When John returned and asked for my help, I then began to talk with him about his

> **The king leads and protects his people by applying wisdom to the war of life.**

life in light of his relationships past and present and in view of the truth of God's Word. I then began to direct him to truth about how to live in a way that was consistent with the deepest passions of his redeemed heart.

> A king does not assure the resolution of a problem; he only offers to lead a person in the path of maturity.

The prophet is a poet who disturbs and arouses hope, the priest is a storyteller who comforts and deepens faith, and the king is a mentor who applies wisdom to life and leads people into war with the weapons of love. For example, the book of Proverbs has been viewed as wisdom taught to young men who were being trained for royal service.

Most of the wisdom books—Proverbs, Song of Songs, Ecclesiastes, and Ruth—are considered to be royal literature. These books are practical, earthy, and not overtly about God. In fact, the books of Ruth and Song of Songs never mention Yahweh. It is not to say that God is not at the foundation of the reflection, but the overt interest is the management of the mystery of life.

A mentor, or a practical instructor, applies truth to life, seeks to help a young man or woman grow through the application of proverbic, wisdom categories to life experience. He passes on common sense and skills, and he monitors the apprentice so he can eventually take over the task related to the field of endeavor.

But the ultimate skill to be taught is how to love. His competence, therefore, is in a distinct area, but even more in developing character to live out the "royal law of love."

## Unity of Offices

Am I a prophet, a priest, a king? In fact, I am all three if I am growing in maturity. It is imperative for me to grow in greater expertise in all three areas. But there is only one who fully reveals what it means to be a prophet, priest, and king. The offices of prophet, priest, and king are fulfilled perfectly in one person: Jesus Christ. Theologian A. A. Hodge reminds us,

It is always to be remembered that these are not three offices, but three

> functions of the one indivisible office of mediator . . . when he [Jesus] teaches, he is essentially a royal and priestly teacher, and when he rules he is a priestly and prophetical king, and when he atones or intercedes he is a prophetical and kingly priest.[3]

He is one, though he fulfills different tasks. The same is to be true of me. I may be more gifted in one area, and that gifting may shape the nature of how I perform my calling, but I must press on to maturity, to be like Christ. I must mature in all three areas if I am to fulfill the task of offering others a picture of Christ. Otherwise, the picture and the task will be perverted. A prophet will become a gnostic; a priest, a charlatan; a king, a despot.

A prophet that does not grow in Christ will be drawn to the complex, the mysterious, and the convoluted twists and turns of the soul. Sadly, this is often seen in psychological jargon that mystifies more than it clarifies. It can lead to a system of thought that only the initiates in the new gnostic faith can comprehend. A prophet must never succumb to obfuscation, hiding behind the poetic at the price of clarity and simplicity.

A priest that does not grow in Christ will be drawn to creating the illusion of a conflict-free community. Sadly, this is often seen in people who banish controversy and conflict in order to say, "peace, peace," when there is no peace. A priest must never hide from the darkness in the heart and community; otherwise it will lead to pretense and snake-oil Christianity.

A king that does not grow in Christ will be drawn to task and order more than people and process. Sadly, this is often seen in dictatorial demands that use blame and shame to control the will of others rather than setting people free to live out their burdens and calling. A king must never lead by force and threat, or he will steal the soul of others for his ill-gotten gain.

## THE CALLING OF A COUNSELOR

Therapy is a small sub-section of the larger task of discipleship. For those who struggle and wish to take a deep and hard look at their heart in light of the great commandment to love the Lord with all their heart, soul, strength, and mind and their neighbor as themselves, then counseling provides an individual and/or group experience to be disrupted, cared for, and directed toward the

> As a counselor I am meant to study the human condition so deeply and so well that I invite others privately and publicly to see who we are meant to be in Christ.

purposes of God. When counseling neglects or denies any of these tasks, then even when it is effective in reducing or restructuring symptoms, it will be less than biblical.

Counseling is an intense, highly focused interaction that allows one person to put aside the formalities and expectations of a "typical" friendship in order to focus on one life (or marriage, or group) and to wrestle with the impediments to growth. Its benefit is found in the context and character of the counselor. The context is based on the supposition of change. Clients come because they want to see change in their lives. Few friendships are based solely on the intentionality of change, nor should they be. But it is appropriate to enter a relationship with a gifted, trained specialist who is equipped to help a person explore the heart, invite trust, and be directed to the war of love. The character of the counselor is formed by the burden that moved her into the work; the training that develops categories for reflection and intervention; and the supervision and experience that hones her heart better to walk the path that she invites others to follow.

Is therapy required for everyone? Is it ever enough? The answer to both is an unequivocal no. We need periods of time set aside for growth. We need to grow in community. And growth in community will always have components of prophetic, priestly, and kingly involvement to draw our heart to God.

Who is best equipped to offer this involvement? The answer is the body of Christ, the church, which is made up of both those with special and general gifts to teach, encourage, and point us toward maturity. Those with special gifts and training are called not only to do the work of the ministry, but also to equip the saints for the labor of revealing Christ.

Therefore, as a counselor I am meant to study the human condition so deeply and so well that I invite others privately and publicly to see who we are in light of what we are meant to be in Christ. A counselor is a connecting, directing prophet that is called to disrupt the body of Christ and invite us all to the rich hope we have in him.

"We" implies community. It necessitates that the trained and called specialist is not to labor in isolation from community. He is to be accountable to others and sensitive to the fact he is not enough for deep and long-lasting change to occur.

We have been most deeply hurt by people, and the hope for healing is equally to occur with people, not just one soul healer. In the next chapter, Dr. Crabb sets forth the place of community as the space for soul change.

# 15

# The Power of Healing Community

⚬⚭⚬

DOES THE WORK OF soul care belong primarily to ordinary Christians in community, with all their weaknesses and imperfections, or is it better handled by professionals in private counseling offices?

We must answer the question thoughtfully. Our answer will significantly influence the direction we take in attempting to minister the gospel to people's lives.

The power to do what needs to be done is there. It's available in the gospel. One answer to the question, however, may release only some of its power, like turning on a faucet halfway. The other answer, if we find the courage to live out its implications, could release waterfalls of power that can carry us to the promised land of purposeful, joyful living.

As Dan has said in the last chapter, the decision is not either-or; it's not a choice between professional therapists or pastoral shepherds. It is rather a question of who is helping whom do their work. Who is the nurse, and who is the doctor? Perhaps a lengthier restatement of the original question will better define the options:

Should the church, expressed in local gatherings, play a supportive role in restoring people's lives while depending on counseling specialists to do the real work of healing? Or is God's design exactly the reverse? Should Christian counselors see themselves as useful participants in a task properly entrusted to the community of saints, to people whose qualification to care for others' souls consists not in their schooling or status but in the depth of their relationship with Christ? And should professional counselors realize that because they work away from the broader community, a great danger lies in their opportunity to bypass the demands of mutual relating and instead to offer more skill than love?

That's the question. It's time to answer it. With the apprehension of the Israelites when they stared at an uncrossable river, I cast my vote for the church. I believe the church can become a healing community with more power to do good in troubled peoples' lives than can ever be available in a counseling center. I continue to esteem my professional colleagues, especially those who see their work as ministry within the body of Christ, and I'm grateful when the power of the gospel is felt in their sessions (and in mine).

But I believe that more power is available to Christians as they relate in ongoing community, and I believe that God designed the local church to do what our culture generally thinks is the job of the counselor. If that is so, then we should push back the limits of what the church can do rather than treating it like merely a helpful support system.

My decision is based on three issues: the nature of problems, the power of community, and God's passion for shepherding. Let me briefly define each one and then spend the rest of the chapter fleshing out my thinking.

## THE NATURE OF PROBLEMS

When we understand who we are and what

goes wrong in our lives, it becomes clear that we are not damaged things that need repair; we are rather disconnected persons that must depend on the gospel to reestablish connection. We are not psychological selves in need of treatment for emotional disorders. We are eternal souls designed for communion with God and with each other, but who have foolishly broken fellowship. The nature of our problems suggests that the power to heal depends on something being first poured into us from another and then poured out of us toward someone else. We do not need an expert doing something to us, like a dentist fixing our teeth. We need to connect closely enough to give and receive from one another.

> We are not damaged things that need repair; we are rather disconnected persons that must depend on the gospel to reestablish connection.

When theologians speak of the relationships that exist among the members of the trinity, they sometimes use the word "perichoresis." This word carries the idea of a close-knit neighborhood where people freely give to one another whatever is needed. When they say that the trinity relates perichoretically, theologians mean that they pour themselves into each other. The Father pours into the Son, the Son into the Father, and so on. Something is given to the other without which each member would not be who he is.

When God created us in his image, he intended that we would similarly pour into one another from the deepest resources of our being. When that pouring takes place, there is connection. Disconnection, I suggest, lies behind most of the problems we take to counselors. Most anorexic girls, for example, have never felt connection with a strong, good person that relieves them of the need to protect what they experience as most fragile within them. When something terrifies them, they find comfort in knowing they are in control of something that might make their world into a kinder, more accepting place. Their need for control is directly proportional to the perceived lack of connection. And it is connection that has the power to deal with those problems.

## THE POWER OF COMMUNITY

The power of theory and technique offers an easy substitute for the strenuous demands of connected relating. Psychotherapy is a one-way relationship that requires less of the person to be successful than a long-term reciprocal relationship requires. The hour-a-week model of helpful relating reduces love to something more manageable than those involved in ongoing community know it to be. Real power is released when we accept the impossible challenge to connect with each other's souls in healing community, a challenge that is minimized in professional settings and maximized in unstructured relationships. The power of the gospel is released when people live with one another in connected community.

More than anything else, we were built to enjoy relationship, the kind the Trinity has always enjoyed and extends to sinful people. When someone gets close enough to see the ugliness inside and refuses either to minimize how bad it is or to shrink from it, when someone believes in us and wisely directs us in releasing the good placed within us by

250

the gospel, then we begin to experience healing.

## THE PASSION FOR SHEPHERDING

The qualification for feeding sheep (and that is the highest calling within our community) is loving Jesus. But the love that qualifies someone to shepherd others develops only when suffering persuades us to give up our self-preserving agendas, when dark nights make Christ's presence necessary (no longer a luxury), when trials make us willing to abandon ourselves fully to Christ because we need him so badly.

The profound intimacy with Christ that only suffering can create enables us to enter other people's lives with the Spirit's healing power. We must be willing to endure the suffering necessary to become shepherds of God's people rather than to settle for training which certifies us as mere therapists. The power of the gospel is most fully released in communities where godly men and women shepherd connected people.

Now, with that quick sketch, let me back up and take another run at it, this time moving a little more slowly.

## WHY I BELIEVE SOUL CARE BELONGS TO THE CHURCH REASON #1: THE NATURE OF OUR PROBLEM

Most of us feel uncomfortable when a friend tells us she is depressed, when a husband worries too much, when a coworker confides in us that his marriage is in trouble, when the older woman who has been discipling us for years admits to a history of drinking problems. Why?

We feel even more uncomfortable when we're doing the sharing, when the problem we're talking about is ours. Again, why?

People feel powerless when they learn of a problem in a friend's life, like a bankrupt man would feel if a buddy down on his luck asked for a loan. We just don't think we have much to offer.

### We Think We Are Impotent

Our culture has sold us on the idea that we really are impotent in the face of most personal problems. When a thirteen-year-old daughter announces to the family that she hates herself, then leaves the dinner table in tears, modern parents immediately worry: Is this evidence of a psychological problem, perhaps the beginning of an eating disorder or clinical depression?

Ideas like that scare us. They make us think that more might be happening than we are equipped to handle. We feel powerless.

People who feel powerless respond in a wide variety of ways to people with problems. They may **attack** ("You shouldn't have these problems. What on earth is the matter with you?"), **moralize** ("If you'd just do what you should, everything would be all right!"), **spiritually mumble** ("Uh, I'm sure God will help. Everything works together for good, you know."), **practice amateur therapy** ("How did you get along with your mother? How do you really feel? What are you afraid to tell me?"), or **give good old-fashioned advice** ("Why don't you court your wife like you did before you got married?").

Those are the kinds of responses we often get when we turn to friends and family for help. Small wonder we schedule time with a counselor. The fact is that most of us are as terrified to enter into the guts of someone else's life (or even our own) as we would be to grab a scalpel and attempt brain surgery.

But why? A good part of the answer is this: We tend to define the nature of per-

253

sonal problems in ways that disempower the community of family and friends.

Think back to the earlier chapters of this book. I suggested that we generally come up with one of six possible explanations for whatever personal problems we experience and that none of the explanations would lead us to depend on the resources of Christian community for help.

Bear with a quick review.

If the cause of our problem is **personal sin**, friends can rebuke, exhort, and provide accountability, but the solution lies in the individual as a choosing, responsible being.

If the cause is rooted in **spiritual deficiency** or **undisciplined living**, others can pray, teach, and direct us toward God and more discipline, but again the real work is done by the individual alone in the presence of God.

If **demonic influence** is behind our problems, then the power of God, perhaps mediated by someone experienced in spiritual warfare, is our only hope.

If **physiological malfunctioning** is involved, appropriate medical experts are needed.

And if unhealthy backgrounds have interacted with our fragile and immature sense

254

of self to generate **psychological problems**, then counseling help seems called for.

## Two Assumptions

I have no quarrel at all with assuming responsibility for dealing with personal sin, seeking God, or disciplining our lives. Spiritual leaders called to confront evil have a legitimate role. Certainly the efforts of physicians and the advances of medical science can be received with gratitude in helping us deal with many of life's problems. And the way Christian communities often operate makes me glad that I can refer folks to caring counselors who will deal biblically with their problems in a safe setting.

My concerns run along two lines. First, in every case, community takes a back seat when it's time to help. And second, when we conclude that problems are psychological, we immediately assume that the trained counselor has more to offer than a Christian community even if that community functions well. To retrieve an earlier metaphor, we treat the community as a water boy and send the broken-armed quarterback to the surgeon.

It's the second line of concern that highlights the debate over whether the church community has within it the resources to powerfully heal or whether we need to turn to the better equipped world of counseling professionals.

Most Christians assume that professionally trained counselors are needed to provide what ordinary Christians cannot provide and they make that assumption because they have bought into two ideas that are rarely challenged:

1. Something is twisted in the human personality that must be identified before it can be straightened, and an expert is best equipped to first recognize then untwist the kinks.

2. Whatever is wrong inside the individual must be dealt with before meaningful involvement with community is possible. Involvement comes after healing; it is not the means of healing.

Let me explore those two ideas.

## Idea #1: Trained Counselors Are Necessary

The first idea claims that trained counselors are necessary to see what problems need to be identified before healing can occur.

Jesus rebuked the Pharisees for believing that they could clean up the outside of their lives without first facing the dirt on the inside (Matthew 23). In an earlier book (*Inside Out*) I argued that the effort to straighten out our lives by merely trying hard to do right would never work, that we must also take an honest look into our hearts and souls. Things are going on in dark places within us that must be admitted and confessed as part of the process of growing toward maturity.

But that raises an important question. Exactly what is it that we must identify, acknowledge as true, and meaningfully deal with? Is it what therapists call "psychological dynamics," that collection of internal impulses, unconscious thoughts, and irrational emotions that reflect both the damage we have endured in our lives and our struggle to cope?

If so, then specialists are necessary. Only they are trained to understand and recognize these things as they skillfully and deeply probe into our lives. They know how to surface what would otherwise remain hidden.

But maybe we have it wrong. Perhaps

what needs to be faced on the inside is more profound and far simpler. I suggest that in order to deal with our problems we need to face two realities present in every human soul:

1. A hunger for connection that, if fully felt, will drive us to God.

2. A stubborn determination to enjoy life without appropriating God's provision for connection.

Those two realities—a hunger for connection with God and a resolve to satisfy that hunger elsewhere—lie at the very center of our souls.

But we have taken those two realities and made things too complicated. We have gone beyond the idea of an image-bearing but fallen soul hungry for God but resistant to him and become enamored with the idea of a psychological self capable of being damaged, abandoned, manipulated, and unwisely defensive on its own behalf.

We no longer call the soul of a person to pursue God and forsake idolatry; instead, we now work to develop a healthier self. That work requires a careful understanding and handling of those psychological dynamics that get in the way of a satisfying experience of one's self. And we sometimes assume that working through those complex dynamics may be essential to worshiping God and loving others well. Hence the need for experts.

But if the internal roots of our personal problems lie simply in our unaroused hunger for God and our unadmitted arrogance that says we don't need him, if dealing with life's problems require that we face these two basic realities of the soul rather than all the complex dynamics of the self, then, I suggest, the community of God's people is back in the healing business.

## Idea #2: Treatment Must Precede Community

The second assumption most people make is that treatment of our problems must precede being in a community; that is, the self must recover before it can give.

To use a simple example: When a man breaks his arm, he must let the surgeon realign the bones and put it in a cast before he can again help his wife button her dress. And the healing process may take weeks, sometimes months, during which time his wife must wear dresses she can button herself.

We assume the same process holds for "personal breaks," that a healing period must be completed before the damaged individual can once again give to others.

> The gospel plants deep within our hearts a desire to give that no amount of pain or sorrow can destroy.

But the gospel plants deep within our hearts a desire to give that no amount of pain or sorrow can destroy. And if it really is more blessed to give than to receive, then healing depends on giving whatever can be given despite the pain rather than understanding the pain and waiting for it to abate.

Steve felt enraged when his wife greeted him after work one evening with a request for more of his time. Job pressures were overwhelming, and he desperately wanted Gloria's sensitivity and support. Instead, she complained about how neglected she felt, and her displeasure lit an angry fire in his stomach. He tried to control his anger, but couldn't. After a ten-minute tirade about her lack of compassion, he slumped in his chair, miserable, unhappy with himself, but feeling justified in what he had said. Gloria left the room in tears.

The next day they spent time with me.

> Steve: Why do I react like that? I really do wish Gloria would be more understanding of my pressures, but I know I'm wrong to yell at her like I did.
>
> Gloria: I get so scared when he's like that. But I never feel Steve's really there for me. If I'm there for him, everything's okay. But if I ask for something that makes him feel like I'm critical, he gets so angry.
>
> Steve: When she met me at the door and told me what she wanted, all I could hear was my mother. She always depended on me for emotional support—Dad was never there—but I could never give her enough. Maybe I feel threatened that if I do try to satisfy Gloria,

I'll fail with her like I always
failed with my mother.

In the office of a psychologist like me,
that conversation could go in a dozen directions, all involving interpretations of the psychological dynamics created by Steve's
background. But the crucial question is this:
Must Steve work through whatever damage
was done to his sense of self by a manipulative mother and absent father? Must he
explore, understand, and work through all
these matters?

Or, because he is a Christian, is there
some desire to bless his wife that survives
his rage and whatever produced it; and can
that desire be aroused and put into action
by recognizing how powerfully he impacts
his wife for good or bad? Rather than merely
trying to control his anger, can he look for
(and assume it's there) a desire to be kind
to his wife that is stronger than his fleshly
desire to harm her? Could that desire be
fanned into a fire if Steve heard God's Spirit
whisper to him, "Steve, I know you love
Christ. I revealed him to you, and you
couldn't keep from loving him. No one who
sees him can. You've been forgiven for all
the wrong you did last night. I believe in

you. You're the Father's choice to love Gloria. And you want to love her with the love you've received through me. Release what I've put in you."

Telling the story of his background could deepen Steve's awareness of his struggles and help Gloria know better how to encourage him. But understanding all the subtle forces that have combined to damage Steve's sense of masculine identity may not be necessary.

If it were, then psychodynamic experts would be necessary. If not, if unreleased love due to unembraced hunger and unacknowledged selfishness (with a denial of its impact) is the problem, then godly Christians who can discern the hunger and selfishness in the soul will be able to powerfully encourage the release of Steve's love toward Gloria.

They can do so by pouring their love and wisdom into Steve, connecting with his soul because they know their own, and drawing out of his heart what God has already put there.

The actual process of pouring would include **profound listening**, the kind of sustained attention that we give only to what we deeply value. When men and women feel valued and meaningfully honored, something stirs within them that longs to be worthy of that respect. Pouring also includes **sensitive discernment**. A godly Christian could gently expose the selfishness of Steve's commitment to never hurt again like he did with his mother by helping him see the pain he is causing his wife today. If Steve's heart has already been changed by the gospel, the awareness of the damage he is causing will awaken a deeper desire to bless Gloria. As that longing surfaces, the godly Christian could further pour into Steve's life by sharing what happens in his (the older Christian's) heart as he sees Steve's longing to give to Gloria. He could make known his excitement over what the miracle of the gospel is enabling Steve to do as he moves toward his wife.

## WHY I BELIEVE SOUL CARE BELONGS TO THE CHURCH REASON #2: THE POWER OF TRUE COMMUNITY

Modern therapeutic culture, which believes that there is more power in therapy than in community, puts its focus on the individual. Although some schools of counseling (for example, systems theory) look carefully at the relational setting in which personal problems occur, most counselors assume that they can do most of what needs to be done by treating problems that exist within the individual. As the client's personal health increases, as he learns to look after his own needs and deal with his own concerns rather than complying with the expectations of others, the assumption is that he will be able to reenter community with a healthy regard for others.

But people who spend time looking after their own needs rarely graduate to altruism. The effort to meet our own needs, once started, is a never-ending process, like pouring buckets of water into our own bottomless well with the promise that when our well fills up, we'll share a bucket with our neighbor.

**People who spend time looking after their own needs rarely graduate to altruism.**

It is one thing to teach that giving to others fills up our own souls. It is quite another to suggest that we must first look after ourselves and when that has been successfully accomplished, we will then give to others.

In commenting on this viewpoint, Allan Bloom, author of *The Closing of the American Mind*, says:

> For us the most revealing and delightful distinction—because it is so unconscious of its wickedness—is between inner-directed and other-directed, with the former taken to be unqualifiedly good. Of course, we are told, the inner-directed person will really care for others. To which I can only respond: if you believe that, you can believe anything.[1]

The philosophy of individualism, in which nothing is more important than an individual's needs and rights, runs today's world, at least in the West. God's deepest passion, however, seems directed not toward individuals (though he numbers the hair on our heads) but toward individuals-in-community. In an excellent book, author Rod Wilson observes:

> The various terms that are used to describe God's people (in the Bible) do not describe the inner dynamics of individuals; rather, they focus on the cor-

porate and communal dimensions. So we read of the people of God, the church of Israel, the commonwealth of Israel, believers, saints, God's household, the family of believers, the body of Christ, fellowship, and disciples.[2]

Certainly God is infinitely concerned for the individual, but his concern is to bring individuals together. Individual fulfillment is never the point. It is the by-product of yielding oneself to the greater good of a community, first the community of the triune God (who is served by receiving glory) and then the community of God's people, the church, whose good is found in growing up into Christ.

As always, Christ is our pattern. As the

God intends that his influence be felt most forcefully through a company of men and women who relate to each other the way God relates.

incarnate Son, he lived to please the Father. As the Lord of his church, he is working to bring all things together. As the Good Shepherd, he goes after one lost sheep to restore it to the flock. Persuading that sheep to come back may require the individual attention of one or more delegates from the flock, but the intention of both shepherd and undershepherds is to return the isolated individual to the company of others where nourishment and protection are available.

God intends that his influence be felt most forcefully through a company of men and women who relate to each other the way God relates. That is where he has chosen to reveal himself, to make known his relational nature which, when seen, calls people who were designed to enjoy perfect relationship to the God who relates perfectly. The divine character in all its fullness (but especially its gracious love) is meant to be on display among those who participate in the divine nature, drawing individuals from communities where God is not visible into communities where he is.

But the plan isn't going too well. Several years ago, Henri Nouwen observed that "our Christian communities are little more than solidarities of well-intentioned people supporting each other in their individual interests."[3] More recently Scott Peck declared that "the church is not only not the body of Christ, it is not even a body, a community. It must become a community before it can serve as the body of Christ."[4]

We have lost the idea that the church is the place where God's power should be most clearly seen and his love most deeply felt. Few people alive today, at least in western culture, have had a real taste of the power of God through community. But many have had a swallow of his power elsewhere: in counselors' offices, at seminars, through books. And that's good. But the most savory hors d'oeuvres before the final banquet are supposed to be passed out in church. Imagine what it would feel like to be really listened to, to experience a discerning eye looking deep into your soul with the twinkling confidence that God's good work will be seen, to enjoy the deepest parts of another being poured into the emptiness of your soul.

But it rarely happens. Local churches have too often become places where people pursuing their own agendas gather to receive encouragement on their individual journeys. When the path gets bumpy, the church is expected to smooth out the bumps or refer individuals to experts who can. The focus is on problems and how to solve them, on a comfortable life (with some meaning thrown in) and how to live it.

Because we have become a nation of individuals-with-problems, we have missed our destiny to be people-in-community. We go to impersonal churches where programs outnumber relationships, and we schedule appointments with personal experts who sell an hour of relationship per week. Our pastors remove themselves from their congregations or are impotent in dealing with them. And our therapists believe that only in the privacy of their offices can people be healed from the damaging effects of the community.

Spiritual leaders who call us to endure

*We have lost the idea that the church is the place where God's power should be most clearly seen and his love most deeply felt.*

problems as we pursue a higher calling than individual comfort are less valued than trained counselors (and compromising pastors) who help us solve whatever problems interfere with personal fulfillment. The result is a weakened community where God's purposes are not pursued, his presence is not deeply enjoyed, and his power is rarely felt. Not many church walls shake in modern times.

One of the reasons for counseling's popularity is its reasonably strong guarantee that someone will like us for an hour. Therapy also affords the opportunity to bare our souls and become meaningfully intimate with a person we'll not have to deal with for the rest of the week. We call that safety and extol it as a virtue. But therapy requires from neither participant—either the

**Because we have become a nation of individuals-with-problems, we have missed our destiny to be people-in-community.**

counselor or the counselee—the depth of character necessary to make it in real community.

I've always felt uncomfortable when clients tell me how well I've loved them. I've never said it, but I've often thought, "For an hour a week, I can put up with anything. Whatever I don't like about you I can overlook for that length of time." It is far easier to love well as a therapist than as a friend. So much less is required. And the pay is better, or at least more immediate.

But the real power to influence lives is not generated by good theory or careful technique. Real power depends on reproducing, in our communities, the kind of relationship enjoyed by the members of the Trinity. Before he died, Jesus prayed that we would be one just as he and the Father were one (John 17:21–23).

Our personal problems are rooted in disconnection, from God because of our arrogance and from others because of our fear and selfishness. The cure is connection. And the power to reconnect depends on our experiencing the gracious relational style of God who loves us when we love another more than him, who forgives us at great personal cost, who believes in us when we fail, and who respects us enough to let us make our own choices. That power is felt when communities of people offer that kind of relationship to each other. (In the next chapter, I suggest what that kind of community might look like.)

## WHY I BELIEVE SOUL CARE BELONGS TO THE CHURCH REASON #3: GOD'S PASSION FOR SHEPHERDING

The story is told of a fourth-century young man who decided to leave the city and join older men in the desert who had given up everything to know God better. His plan was to be mentored by these desert fathers, as they were known, and to then return to the city with the power to help others know God more fully.

When he first arrived in the desert, he sought out the most revered of the desert fathers and asked him this question, "What is required for me to most powerfully influence my culture for Christ?"

The old man paused, not to gather his thoughts (he already knew what answer he would give) but rather to ponder whether the young man could hear what he was about to say. Finally he spoke: "Never answer a question that the quality of your life has not provoked someone to ask."

Those words are difficult to hear. Perhaps the young man understood their implications. Modern culture does not.

We ask our most important questions of people who are credentialed to answer them. We live in the day of experts, people whose qualifications to help us with life's struggles have more to do with degrees than character, more to do with experience in handling problems than with depth in knowing Christ, more to do with training at an institution which accepts students on the basis of their grade point average than with a calling to direct people to Christ confirmed by others similarly called.

## The Office of Elder

A grave symptom of our illness is that we have learned to discount the office of church elder as a position filled by well-off, well-connected, or managerial-type men. The word "elder," when spoken in the context of church life, creates the image of a good man (rarely a woman) whom we trust to handle the business of the church but would never trust to deal with the issues of our souls. How many fathers whose teenage sons are doing drugs turn to the elders of their church for help? How many wives whose husbands struggle with pornography ask for time to meet with a church elder? How many people suffering from memories of sexual abuse make known their burdens to a member of the elder board?

Not many. And I don't blame them. Too often, requests for help with hard personal matters would be met with poorly disguised panic in the elder's eyes or with an attempt to help too quickly. The quick attempt to help is probably the harder of the two to handle. It says, "I don't take you seriously. I'm unwilling to get involved in the real struggles of your soul. You really don't need that level of connection. If you would just do such-and-such you'd be fine. And if you think you need more, see a therapist."

For decades, hurting people have found more help in counselors' offices than with church elders.

That is the way it is, but it is not the way it is supposed to be.

One day God looked down on his lonely, terrified people, and he spoke sharply to their spiritual leaders. "'Woe to the shepherds who are destroying and scattering the sheep of my pasture!' declares the LORD . . . 'I will place shepherds over them who will tend them, and they will no longer be afraid or terrified, nor will any be missing,' declares the LORD" (Jeremiah 23:1, 4).

**Hurting people have found more help in counselors' offices than with church elders.**

Notice the phrase "of my pasture." God provides the nourishment our souls need when our kids rebel, when our husbands are immoral, when memories of abuse haunt our sleep. God provides the nourishment of encouragement to go on, wisdom to know what to do, and power to love well and to rest. But he calls shepherds to direct people to those pastures and to help them find the nourishment God provides.

We have reached a strange state of affairs. The appointed shepherds of the church direct its ministries from the ivory tower of "elders' meetings," approving budgets, hiring staff, overseeing youth programs, while Christian counselors get involved in people's lives in their suburban offices, hearing their stories, sharing their pain, and bringing the gospel to bear on their lives. Elders manage the business of the church, while experts do the work of shepherding.

Certainly some elders meaningfully shepherd and, regrettably, some Christian counselors do little that could be called Christlike shepherding. But after twenty-five years as a professional therapist and trainer of counselors for fourteen, I have concluded that more shepherding goes on in counseling offices than in churches. And yet when a good professional biblical counselor counsels, he or she is coming closer to what the Bible means by shepherding than by what our culture understands to be expert professional treatment. But shepherding properly belongs to the church community.

If that's true, then our response should be twofold: (1) to thank God for faithful Christian counselors who serve the body of Christ through their profession, and (2) to do whatever we can to restore shepherding to the Christian community, where it could have even more power than in counselors' offices.

## The True Elder

Every believer is called to connect with fellow believers, to enter their lives, to see

God at work, and to touch them with the passion of Christ. But certain believers, often those whose sensitive natures have made them feel more heavily the weight of life, have been specially prepared by God to enter, see, and touch with unusual power. These folks are the true elders in the body.

In their dependence on Christ, these people have been so filled with his heart and mind that they can enter more deeply, see more clearly, and touch with more passionate wisdom than many others. These are the ones who can shepherd God's people.

But where are they? Often sitting unnoticed in the back row of church, undervalued because they have no counseling degree, too self-effacing to claim humility as the basis for entering into people's lives, preferring rather to retreat. They are men and women who could be released to shepherd if:

1. They understood the nature of people's problems in a way that persuaded them they do have something to offer.
2. They enjoyed meaningful connection in their communities where the qual-

ity of their lives was noticed enough to arouse questions in others.

3. They were equipped by current shepherds to understand the biblical categories of the spiritual life and human functioning well enough to enter deeply, see wisely, and touch passionately.

4. They assumed responsibility for the small portion of the flock entrusted to their care (1 Peter 5:3) rather than trying to help too many, which neither time nor opportunity allows.

Cases requiring social control or extended involvement or medical assistance may require what only professionals are in a position to provide. But rather than referring too quickly to experts, I suggest we think hard about how spiritual leadership can involve itself with a community (that properly values connection) to deal with the painful realities of people's lives.

In the world as it is, people who turn to the church for help cannot realistically expect to find what counselors can more often provide. But in the world as it could be, people would turn to their Christian communities and find connection that nourishes their souls. And they would experience shepherding that guides them to live the abundant life of enjoying the way Christ relates and imitating him well in their relationships with others.

# 16

# What Connected Community Looks Like

⸙

THE GOSPEL RECONNECTS PEOPLE. It brings together folks whose selfishness has isolated them by first providing forgiveness for their selfishness and then empowering them to better relate to others, to give themselves to others the same way the members of the Trinity give themselves to each other. The gospel reconnects people to God and to others.

We are called to reflect "trinitarian-style" relating in human community. And we can move in that direction only when we stop seeing ourselves as damaged selves needing repair by a counseling expert and realize that we are isolated souls who can find life only through connection with God and with other people. "Gospel communities" aim toward the vision of deepened connection. They believe that their biggest problem is disconnection, and they trust the power of the gospel to overcome it.

> "Gospel communities" aim toward the vision of deepened connection.

But what does a gospel community look like? Exactly how do they relate? Do they share lots of feelings? Do they openly confront sin in each other? Do they focus on the nature of their relationships at any given moment, making known how others make them feel and what they are experiencing?

Or do they say only spiritual things to one another and keep their distance from any shameful emotion or troubling conflict that might disturb pleasant interactions?

How do people who are living in the power of the gospel relate? That's the question for this chapter.

282

The beginning of the answer lies in an issue I've already mentioned. Gospel communities do not look at their members as damaged selves whose hope for healing lies more in professional treatment than in nourishing community. They see themselves as naturally inclined toward a self-preoccupation that disconnects them from others. They view people as isolated souls whose central hope is found in connection. And they trust the gospel, not only to forgive their selfishness, but also to create within them a new inclination to put God first and to give what they have to others. Gospel communities nourish that inclination in their members, exposing and removing obstacles that stand in their way and thrilling over any expression of the holy passions of a regenerate heart.

Gospel communities don't repair people, they nourish them. They don't depend on trained specialists to fix something broken. They depend rather on godly Christians to nourish what God's Spirit has placed within every believer and to encourage the release of those Christlike urges toward others.

Gospel communities build their relational lives around three principles.

# PRINCIPLE #1: THE GOOD IS MORE POWERFUL THAN THE BAD

Through the power of the gospel, God has placed something good in each of our hearts that is more powerful than all that is bad.

> *Gospel communities don't repair people, they nourish them.*

That "something good" is a longing to connect, with God in worship and obedience and with others in loving service. The new covenant described in Ezekiel 36:25–27 and Jeremiah 31:33–34 creates within us the inclination to relate to others the way the members of the Trinity relate within their perfect community. The text in Ezekiel reads: "And I will put my Spirit in you and move you to follow my decrees and be careful to keep my laws" (36:27). God is not forcing us to live correctly; he is moving us to live out his decrees and laws which always reflect his eternal character as a perfectly relational God.

Often, this longing to connect surfaces most clearly when we face how severely our bad urges have harmed people we love. When my wife recently told me that she sometimes feels more useful than honored, I began to see how stubbornly I demand that she come through for me when I'm struggling. When I hurt, it seems so reasonable to want her to do something for me that will help. When that desire is dominant, it is bad. But because it seems so legitimate (after all, I'm not really asking for much), I have a hard time recognizing it as bad—until I see the pain it causes my wife.

Then I become aware of another desire within me, a longing to bless my wife. At this point, the spirit-flesh tussle becomes pronounced. The battle begins in earnest. Will I repent of the demand that my wife soothe my ache, knowing the debilitating pressure my demand creates in her? Will I release the longing to bless? Will I stop requiring anything of her and choose rather to give something to her? The struggle between the flesh (my bad longing) and the spirit (my good longing) often feels like an encounter between David and Goliath. I must remember that the slingshot in my hand is a weapon from God that can indeed slay the giant.

Gospel communities believe in their people. They know the gospel has actually created within forgiven hearts good passions that can be nourished and released. And they know that all the bad urges generated by abuse, betrayal, and rejection are not able to overcome what God inclines his people to do.

## PRINCIPLE #2: WE MUST RELEASE OUR GOOD PASSIONS

Our own souls are most deeply nourished when we release our good urges, when we give to others even when everything in us is screaming to get.

In Acts 20:35, the apostle Paul told us that Jesus himself said, "It is more blessed to give than to receive."

Remember my earlier discussion of "perichoresis," a word that describes how the members of the Trinity relate among themselves. In a word, they give. The Father pours himself into the Son, the Son pours himself into the Father, and so on. And when one pours into the other, nothing is lost in the one who is giving. Rather than losing anything, the one who gives experiences the deep joy that only loving can bring.

It's like that in human community. The act of giving itself provides the nourishment our souls desire. God's design for marriage illustrates this point. A husband physically pours himself into his wife, and new life emerges. The one who pours loses nothing, the one who receives becomes what she could not be apart from another pouring into her, and the two of them become one, united as parents who enjoy the fruit of their connection.

Some months ago I was walking through an especially dark valley. Words had been said to me that cut me to the core. At lunch one day with my wife and good friends, I made known my hurt. They all listened, fully engaged with what I was saying. Then Bill leaned forward and, with tears in his eyes and his jaw set firmly, said, "I never want you to again have to endure that sort of thing alone."

Immediately, I felt new life arising in my soul. My friend was in the pains of labor on my behalf, wanting to see Christ's comfort and strength more deeply formed in me in the middle of my trial.

> The act of giving itself provides the nourishment our souls desire.

Two things happened. One, I felt energized. I didn't want to retreat, to hide in a corner away from the possibility of further hurt. Nor did I want to get even. I wanted to face this situation and handle it well, to give what Christ would give. The sun peeked over the horizon.

Two, my friend felt alive, not proud, not condescending, but alive. Connected. Powerful. He had given from deep parts within him to a friend. He was blessed. What he accomplished in five minutes would thrill a therapist if it took twenty sessions to achieve.

## PRINCIPLE #3: GIVING THRIVES IN COMMUNITY

Finally, I would argue that the urge to give dies in a culture of individualism, but it thrives in connected community.

When we focus on resolving our problems through an exploration of ourselves, we rarely get in touch with the longing to bless that God's Spirit has created within us. When a client enters a counseling office to solve her problems, to feel better about herself, to relieve distressing symptoms, unless the counselor turns the focus toward her calling to contribute within community, she may

288

never identify and release her urge to give. The Spirit may remain quenched.

But when people understand that we each need to do our part in building up the body of Christ, then we're bothered by our own selfishness and failure to give. Instead of focusing on our own problems, we focus on how we have hurt others. That crushing realization breaks our stubbornness and, like the flask of perfume that releases its fragrance only when it's shattered, our souls begin to release the lovely desire to bless.

## ENTER, SEE, AND TOUCH

Gospel communities feed on these three principles. They know that the desire to give can be stronger in redeemed hearts than the demand to get. They rejoice in the opportunity to give, realizing that giving to others what Christ has already given to them provides nourishment for their own souls. Everything they do reflects the value they place on connection. They know that individualism, that approach to life that puts me above you, is lethal, and they also know that connecting in community provides the richest opportunity to grow in the grace of Christ.

Perhaps we need to put more energy into developing a vision for community than into refining our theories of counseling. To do this, I will offer a simple sketch of trinitarian community as it could be imitated in our relationships within the body of Christ. The sketch includes three elements: enter, see, and touch.

## Enter

Listen so profoundly that people who tell you their stories begin to believe that whatever matters to them matters to you. Help them to believe it because it's true. Remember that you cannot deeply enter someone's life as a judge or critic, or even as an advisor. Don't be eager to pounce on sin or to correct error, but rather come to people excited by a vision of what they will become as Christ forms himself in them (Galatians 4:19).

## See

Look in others for what you've already seen in yourself, both good and bad, nothing more, nothing less. Remember that the power to see clearly into another's heart depends on first seeing into your own. Expect to see two core realities, a hunger for God that energizes the passion to worship and love, and a terrified determination to protect themselves from further hurt by connecting with no one, a determination that leaves people looking for satisfaction in pleasure they can control.

## Touch

Most people have never felt close-up what it's like to relate with Christ. Make it your priority to know Christ well enough to experience the thrill of enjoying perfect love. Pay whatever price is required for that inestimable treasure. Then, with a vision for what people could become when they enjoy that same kind of relationship, believe that nothing that has ever happened to them and that nothing they have ever done can overcome God's power in changing their character. With a sense of privilege and calling, touch them with your passion for Christ as it is reflected in the way you handle your failures, battles, victories, and joys. Ask God to arouse in them a hunger to know Christ, the same hunger that drives you in all you do.

## THE POWER OF COMMUNITY

The great need of our day is the empowerment of ordinary Christians. You don't need to be a trained counselor to make a difference. You may be only a water boy on the football field, but perhaps water is what's most needed. The water of life has the power not only to slake thirst but also to heal broken bones, to reconnect members of the body into loving community.

There is power in community. It is the power of connection, of entering someone's life with the energy of Christ, of seeing someone's heart with the mind of Christ, of touching someone's soul with the love of Christ. That's what gospel communities look like.

And when they function properly, when the power of community is released, good things happen. The last chapter discusses what we can hope for, what really could happen when we experience connection.

# 17

# So What Is Our Hope?

<br>

⟨❧⟩

<br>

ONE QUESTION REMAINS, THE last—
and perhaps most important—of the four
questions that hurting people ask: Exactly
what can we hope for if we decide to get
help for our problems?

What can the heartbroken parents of a
rebellious nineteen-year-old son hope for?
He smokes pot, sleeps with his girlfriend,
and makes enough money to live in a run-
down apartment with three other rebels.
Occasionally, he meets his parents for church,
usually unshaven and with glazed eyes.
They're talking with a counselor, a specialist in adolescent problems. The son, of
course, will not go. What can the parents
hope for?

What can the middle-aged woman who feels betrayed by her pastor hope for? She confided in him about some difficulties with her marriage, nothing all that serious. During their second appointment, he sat next to her on the sofa in his office rather than in the chair across the room. She felt uncomfortable and did not schedule a third meeting.

Within days, the church grapevine faithfully carried the news that her flirtatious ways were causing problems in her marriage. Her husband was furious. He stormed into the pastor's office to confront him. The pastor denied any wrongdoing, either sexual advance or gossip, and hinted that the gentleman's wife might be struggling with severe emotional problems. She slipped into depression and went to see a therapist. What can she hope for?

What can the young man caught up in pornography hope for? No one knows about his habit. He lives by himself, makes good money in the early stages of a promising insurance career, is a newly appointed deacon, leads a midweek Bible study for singles, stays in great physical shape, and, not surprisingly, is considered a highly eligible bachelor. He's had more than one invitation for dinner to an older couple's home who just happened to have a daughter about his age.

But he hates himself. He feels like a phony. The tension of a divided life—the public one that looks nearly perfect and the private one filled with magazines and videos he vows to resist but never does—is ripping him up. He has vowed to come clean with someone. But who? A friend? His pastor? A therapist? And when he does, what can he hope for?

## SOLVING PROBLEMS IS NOT ENOUGH

Some problems disappear or at least diminish with medication. Restoring chemical balance to the body's system can have dramatically gratifying effects. Depressions lift, anxiety reduces, energy returns, obsessions lessen, motivation increases. My reaction when this happens? I praise God, the same way I praise him when a dentist makes a toothache go away or a mechanic starts a stalled car.

For many people, a good dose of responsible living helps. Life becomes more manageable (or at least less overwhelming) when they take hold of themselves and become more disciplined and moral, when they

It's tempting to declare that we can improve the quality of our lives through medicine, discipline, personal holiness, spiritual warfare, and a directed pursuit of God.

deal with laziness, sloppy personal habits, and sinful patterns that for too long have gone unchecked.

Others report the benefits of waging direct war against the devil. Bonds of self-hatred and sexual addiction are broken, the sun begins to shine again in dark places of the soul, and grateful Christians testify that God's power has liberated them from demonic enslavement.

More and more spiritually hungry westerners are finding a quietness of heart they've never before known through religious exercises practiced for centuries in the East, exercises like contemplative prayer and silent retreats. Men and women who call themselves spiritual directors are offering their services to guide people into new experiences of God. Therapists sometimes refer their clients to spiritual directors. Occasionally, a therapist becomes a spiritual director.

It's tempting to look at the good that is being done in all these ways and to declare that this is our hope, that we can improve the quality of our lives through medicine, discipline, an increased commitment to personal holiness, spiritual warfare, and a directed pursuit of God. And all these measures are part of our hope, because they do help, often generating desirable effects.

It's dangerous, of course, to affirm something as good simply because of its enjoyable consequences. Leaving a shrewish wife for a cooperative mistress will likely be a pleasant experience, but that fact doesn't justify the choice.

But this world is so full of misery and struggle that I find myself grateful for whatever measures offer real help provided that (1) they don't violate biblical morality and teaching, (2) they don't weaken a commitment to endure hardship for the cause of Christ, and (3) they don't erode our dependence on the Spirit to make us like Christ, or our consuming desire that it happen. When people are helped by taking antidepressant medication, by eating healthier and jogging more, by becoming scrupulously honest in their business dealings, by telling the devil to scat, or by spending more time in prayer, I say great.

## OUR GREATEST HOPE

But, and there is a but, sometimes all these good things don't seem to provide the hope that hurting people need. Some struggles don't seem to be affected by these measures: struggles like worry over circumstances, over health or finances or people we love; distress over tangled relationships, like in a gossiping church community, where there is no clear solution; and agony over personal battles against lust or alcoholism that continue despite our prayers and good resolutions.

Many of our problems are uniquely human problems, that is, they reflect our struggle to live as people who were meant to enjoy perfect community in a world where there is none. And these problems will not be addressed richly or deeply apart from community. Until the sufferer deals with his problems in a relationship with someone else, there is really no hope.

With all of its imperfections, the community of God's people does provide the resources we need to live with purpose and meaning in this alien world. Whether community is offered by an individual or by a small group, the simple truth is that we need to be living with other people whom we know and who know us, folks we receive from and give to.

If we give up on community—and who has not been tempted to do so—we give up on life. Even though many of our worst problems began in bad community, our hope still lies in community.

**Precisely because our worst problems began in community, that's where our hope lies.**

Let me say it again more strongly: Precisely because our worst problems began in community, that's where our hope lies. There is a principle running through life that says whatever has the greatest potential to do harm has an equal potential to do good.

God designed us to thrive in community. Our souls were crafted to find their nourishment in receiving from others and in giving to others. When good is poured back and forth, we live. When bad is exchanged, we die. That fact reflects the nature of our trinitarian Creator, a God who himself lives in an eternal community of three persons who always pours sheer love into one another.

Now the good news is that a little bit of shared goodness has more power to bless us than a lot of shared badness has to harm us. We don't have to have a perfect community to enjoy its benefits. But we do have to be connected by hearts that love God, that are growing in wisdom, and that live increasingly in the power of the gospel.

## WHAT HOPE IS NOT

Our hope is in community. Sometimes that community will be most experienced in a counselor's office, sometimes over lunch, sometimes with a group of folks watching a movie together, sometimes in a small group Bible study or in a recovery group.

But what exactly is this hope? It is not that things will always go our way. Connected souls don't always make enough money to pay their bills. They get cancer like anyone else. Their children might break their hearts. Community, even when offered by a profes-

300

sional counselor who specializes in family therapy, does not guarantee that the prodigal will return home.

Nor is our hope that we will always feel the way we want to feel. Some depressions won't lift.

John Phillips, the English writer of a generation ago, cheered thousands of people through his personal correspondence and far more through his books while he himself stayed depressed through most of his life. Godly men and women sometimes struggle with perverted sexual urges right up to their deathbeds and leave this world (as every right-thinking person must do) depending on God's grace to bring them home. There *is* victory over the habit of sin. However, there may not be victory over the presence of sin as a powerful force that is sometimes overwhelming, a force to which we may sometimes yield.

And our hope is not that psychological symptoms will always disappear. Sometimes they do, perhaps through therapy or medication or a good Sunday school class. But not always. Nervous tics might continue despite prescription drugs. Eating habits may remain troublesome and the wounds from sexual abuse may still ache despite extensive therapy. Sleep disturbances may continue after neurological examinations and in spite of spiritual exercises and warm milk before retiring.

## WHAT HOPE IS

So what is our hope? Simply this: That nothing, no problem in our circumstances or in our souls, can keep us from living out God's purpose for our lives if we are abandoned to him. If cancer blocks that purpose, it will be removed. If depression gets in the way, it will lift. If fatigue from poor sleep keeps us from fulfilling God's agenda, we'll snore with the best of them. If wealth is part of the plan, we'll close the big deal.

But when illness, discouragement, prodigal children, insomnia, and money struggles are useful to God in advancing his purposes, they will be a part of our lives. We are not wrong to take whatever honorable measures we can to alleviate our suffering, and we are not wrong to thank God if things improve. But, because we cannot always understand what God is up to, we are wrong to demand less suffering, to make it our top priority to change things to be the way we would like.

Hope for distraught parents lies in their

confidence in a loving God's good and just plan, a confidence strengthened when friends stand by them without offering solutions. It lies in their capacity to still give to their child and to others the love that has the power to turn hearts toward Christ, a capacity most fully released when others give that love powerfully to them.

Hope for the person caught in tangled relationships where nothing is clear consists in the opportunity to connect with at least a few people in the middle of ongoing battles with betrayal, resentment, and fear. Nourishment from a few others can reduce our obsessive concerns to handle every tension properly without diminishing our desire to reflect Christ.

Hope for the man losing the struggle with sexual temptation can be found in the good heart that remains within him despite his failures, a good heart that wants to bless others. As he enters into the miracle of "Christ in him" and releases his longing to give what God has uniquely placed within

**Life in Christ, together: that's our hope.**

him, he will discover that godly affections are stronger than ungodly ones, that the joy of living in community can be more powerful than the urge to view another video. As he walks in the Spirit, he will not fulfill the lusts of the flesh.

Problems that get in the way of God's agenda for us can be overcome through the power of the gospel made real through community. The struggles that remain become opportunities for deeper trust.

In the middle of our difficult lives, the gospel of Jesus Christ builds a bridge between us and God and between us and other people. As we learn to walk across that bridge, to connect with God and with his people, we will come alive. Struggles will continue, but they will be nudged out of the center of our lives by the reality of meaning, joy, perseverance, and love. Life in Christ, together: that's our hope.

# Epilogue

FEW MEN HAVE MEANT to me what Dan Allender has meant. He says the same thing about me.

He was with me when I received the hardest news of my life. His compassion and strength ministered deeply to me.

I was with him when he was told his father was dying. Never have I felt so inadequate as I prayed with him that night in Vienna—nor so sincere.

Our history of friendship is long—nearly twenty years—and rich. For reasons neither of us clearly understands, God has led us to move into separate spheres of ministry. We feel the loss keenly. We find ourselves emphasizing different elements in our approach

305

to helping people. But we stand together on the foundation of the gospel and God's Word.

And we stand together as brothers, not partnering as we once did, but as men whose hearts are warmly bound by history, by common convictions, and by a love that wants only God's richest blessings for each other's lives.

As you read this book, particularly the last section, you will notice some of our differing approaches. Dan continues to pursue his vision (and mine) of seeing godly men and women deepen their understanding of the soul and of the call to imitate Christ. His specific burden is to train mature believers to counsel in an academic context. But I sense God's calling to encourage the church to connect more deeply and to shepherd more powerfully, to see godly people within the church become "elders of the soul."

We're both advocates of counseling, and we're both committed to the work of the local church. We want to see ourselves and others more and more conformed to the image of Christ. We have a few different ideas on how best to get there, but we both want the same thing.

We write this book not to encourage division or debate between camps, but to stimulate thoughts; and to firmly hold hands as together we proclaim that there is hope for the hurting, that every problem in life finds its ultimate resolution in the gospel of Jesus Christ.

# Notes

CHAPTER 8

1. I am indebted to Rod Wilson for some of the ideas in this chapter. See Rod Wilson, *Counseling and Community* (Dallas: Word, 1995).

CHAPTER 10

1. For a more extensive exploration of the controversy regarding the false memory syndrome and the nature of memory, see Dan B. Allender, *The Wounded Heart* (Colorado Springs, Colo.: NavPress, 1990).

CHAPTER 12

1. David Powlison, *Power Encounters* (Grand Rapids, Mich.: Baker, 1995), 29.
2. Ibid., 30.

## CHAPTER 14

1. Richard F. Lovelace, *Dynamics of Spiritual Life: An Evangelical Theology of Renewal* (Downers Grove, Ill.: InterVarsity Press, 1979), 88–89.

2. See Tremper Longman III and Daniel G. Reid, *God Is a Warrior* (Grand Rapids, Mich.: Zondervan, 1995) and Dan B. Allender and Tremper Longman III, *Bold Love* (Colorado Springs, Colo.: NavPress, 1992).

3. A. A. Hodge, *Outlines of Theology* (London: The Banner of Truth Trust, 1972), 395.

## CHAPTER 15

1. Allan Bloom, *The Closing of the American Mind* (New York: Simon and Schuster, 1987), 178.

2. Rod Wilson, *Counseling and Community* (Waco, Tex.: Word, 1995), 71. This was perhaps the most significant book I read in preparing for this chapter.

3. Henri J. M. Nouwen, *Clowning in Rome: Reflections on Solitude, Celibacy, Prayer, and Contemplation* (Garden City, New York: Image, 1979), 9.

4. M. Scott Peck, *The Different Drum: Community Making and Peace* (New York: Touchstone, 1988), 300. Quoted in Wilson, ibid., xiii.

# About the Authors

Dr. Larry Crabb is a well-known conference and seminar speaker and popular author. He is Distinguished Scholar-in-Residence at Colorado Christian University in Morrison, Colorado. He has written numerous best-selling books, including *Finding God*, which is also available in Large Print from Walker & Company. With Dr. Dan Allender, he is the coauthor of *Encouragement*. The parents of two grown sons, he and his wife, Rachael, live outside of Denver.

Dr. Dan Allender is the founder of Wounded Heart Ministries, a nationwide speaking and teaching ministry. He also maintains a private counseling practice in Denver and is the author of many books. He and his wife, Rebecca, are the parents of three children and live in Littleton, Colorado.

Walker & Company Large Print books
are available from your local bookstore.
Please ask for them.
If you want to receive a catalog of our titles,
send your name and address to:

Beth Walker
Walker & Company
435 Hudson Street
New York, New York 10014

Look for these latest Large Print titles from
Walker & Company

### The Bible Cure
Reginald Cherry, M.D.

### Christmas Stories for the Heart
compiled by Alice Gray

### Death and the Life After
Billy Graham

### Experiencing God
Henry T. Blackaby & Claude V. King

### Friends Through Thick & Thin
Gloria Gaither, Sue Buchanan,
Peggy Benson, Joy MacKenzie

### The Gift of Forgiveness
Charles Stanley

### Strengthening Your Grip
Charles Swindoll

Among the many other titles available are:

### Abiding in Christ
Cynthia Heald

### And the Angels Were Silent
Max Lucado

### Apples of Gold
Jo Petty

### The Best of Catherine Marshall
edited by Leonard LeSourd

### The Blood
Benny Hinn

### A Book of Angels
Sophy Burnham

### Book of Hours
Elizabeth Yates

### Breakfast with Billy Graham

### Brush of an Angel's Wing
Charlie W. Shedd

### Encourage Me
Charles Swindoll

**15 Minutes Alone with God**
Emilie Barnes

**Finding God**
Larry Crabb

**Finding God in Unexpected Places**
Philip Yancey

**Footprints**
Margaret Fishback Powers

**A Gathering of Hope**
Helen Hayes

**Getting Through the Night**
Eugenia Price

**God Came Near**
Max Lucado

**Golden Treasury of Psalms and Prayers**
Edna Beilenson

**Good Morning, Holy Spirit**
Benny Hinn

**The Grace Awakening**
Charles Swindoll

**The Greatest Story Ever Told**
Fulton Oursler

# The Guideposts Treasury of Christmas

## Heaven: Your Real Home
Joni Eareckson Tada

## The Hiding Place
Corrie ten Boom

## Hinds' Feet on High Places
Hannah Hurnard

## Hope and Faith for Tough Times
Robert Schuller

## Hope for the Troubled Heart
Billy Graham

## How to Handle Adversity
Charles Stanley

## I Am with You Always
G. Scott Sparrow

## I've Got to Talk to Somebody, God
Marjorie Holmes

## The Jesus I Never Knew
Philip Yancey

## The Joyful Journey
Clairmont, Johnson, Meberg, Swindoll

**Just As I Am**
Billy Graham

**Keep a Quiet Heart**
Elisabeth Elliot

**Killing Giants, Pulling Thorns**
Charles Swindoll

**The Knowledge of the Holy**
A. W. Tozer

**The Lady, Her Lover, and Her Lord**
T. D. Jakes

**Laugh Again**
Charles Swindoll

**A Layman Looks at the Lord's Prayer**
W. Phillip Keller

**Letters to My Grandchildren**
Charlie W. Shedd

**Lord, Teach Me to Pray**
Kay Arthur

**Mere Christianity**
C. S. Lewis

**More Than a Carpenter**
Josh McDowell

**No Wonder They Call Him the Savior**
Max Lucado

**On the Anvil**
Max Lucado

**A Path Through Suffering**
Elisabeth Elliot

**The Power of Positive Thinking**
Norman Vincent Peale

**Prayers and Promises for Every Day**
Corrie ten Boom

**The Pursuit of Holiness**
Jerry Bridges

**Readings for Meditation and Reflection**
C. S. Lewis

**Six Hours One Friday**
Max Lucado

**The Source of My Strength**
Charles Stanley

**Stories for the Heart**
Alice Gray

**Strength to Love**
Martin Luther King Jr.

**This Is Your Day for a Miracle**
Benny Hinn

**Three Steps Forward, Two Steps Back**
Charles Swindoll

**To Help You Through the Hurting**
Marjorie Holmes

**To Mother With Love**
Helen Steiner Rice

**A Touch of His Freedom**
Charles Stanley

**A Touch of His Wisdom**
Charles Stanley

**A Treasury of Christmas Classics**

**What Happens to Good People
When Bad Things Happen**
Robert Schuller

**Where Is God When It Hurts?**
Philip Yancey

**The Wonderful Spirit-Filled Life**
Charles Stanley